AMERICAN
SILVER EAGLES
A GUIDE TO THE
U.S. BULLION COIN PROGRAM
THIRD EDITION

John M. Mercanti
with Michael "Miles" Standish

Foreword by Michael Reagan

Whitman Publishing, LLC
PUBLISHING SINCE 1934

www.whitman.com

AMERICAN
SILVER EAGLES
A GUIDE TO THE U.S. BULLION COIN PROGRAM
THIRD EDITION

www.whitman.com

© 2016 Whitman Publishing, LLC
3101 Clairmont Road • Suite G • Atlanta, GA 30329

ISBN: 0794844073
Printed in China

Disclaimer: No warranty or representation of any kind is made concerning the accuracy or completeness of the information presented, or its usefulness in purchases or sales. The opinions of others may vary. The author and consultants may buy, sell, and sometimes hold certain of the items discussed in this book.

Caveat: The price estimates given are subject to variation and differences of opinion. Certain rare coins trade infrequently, and an estimate or past auction price may have little relevance to future transactions. Before making decisions to buy or sell, consult the latest information. Coin grading is subject to wide interpretation, and opinions can differ, sometimes widely, even with coins certified by grading services. Past performance of the any item in the market is not necessarily an indication of future performance, as the future is unknown. Such factors as changing demand, popularity, grading interpretations, emergence of hoards, new discoveries, strength of the overall market, and economic conditions will continue to be influences. The market value for a given coin can fall or it can rise.

If you enjoy the behind-the-scenes history, market analysis, and colorful illustrations of *American Silver Eagles*, you will also enjoy *American Gold and Platinum Eagles: A Guide to the U.S. Bullion Coin Programs* (by Edmund C. Moy) and *American Gold and Silver: U.S. Mint Collector and Investor Coins and Medals, Bicentennial to Date* (by Dennis Tucker).

Whitman Publishing is a leader in the antiques and collectibles field. For a complete catalog of numismatic reference books, supplies, and storage and display products, visit Whitman Publishing online at www.Whitman.com.

CONTENTS

CONTRIBUTORS

Ira & Larry Goldberg Coins & Collectibles contributed photographs of half cents from the 1790s. Stack's Bowers Galleries contributed various images from its auction archives. The U.S. Mint contributed images from its archives. Certain images were used, with permission, from the *Guide Book of United States Coins*. The Ronald Reagan Presidential Library shared the photograph on page x. Steve Lovegrove photographed the Liberty Walking half dollar in chapter 1. James Mundie and the Samuel S. Fleisher Art Memorial shared the image of the Frank Gasparro relief medallion in chapter 2. PCGS contributed the bullion coin images used in chapter 3. The portrait of author John Mercanti in appendix A is by Andrew Harrer / Bloomberg, via Getty Images. Heath MacAlpine contributed photographs of some of the medals pictured in appendix A.

Q. David Bowers reviewed the manuscript, offered suggestions, and shared photographs relating to U.S. Mint chief engraver Frank Gasparro, Adolph A. Weinman, and others. Troy Thoreson reviewed the manuscript and offered suggestions. PCGS contributed certified-coin population data.

Certain essays within this book were written by Whitman Publishing staff.

Michael "Miles" Standish contributed to the first and second editions of this book. Standish was the first full-time coin grader at the Professional Coin Grading Service (PCGS). He currently serves as a vice president at Numismatic Guaranty Corporation of America (NGC). His career began in 1984 as an authenticator for the ANA Certification Service. He has championed the market for modern U.S. coins, developed innovative coin-packaging concepts, advised dealers and hobbyists, presented expert testimony at trial, and mentored young numismatists. For his service to the hobby community and to the U.S. Mint, in 2011 Standish was awarded a Director's Coin for Excellence medal by Edmund C. Moy.

Steve Roach contributed to the update of the third edition of *American Silver Eagles*. Roach has been deeply involved with numismatics for more than 20 years, starting as a young collector in Michigan. He is a Certified Member of the International Society of Appraisers. Two years spent as a coin grader and nearly three years at a major coin wholesaler have given him a rich understanding of the hobby, its markets, and the unique personalities and exceptional objects that make collecting meaningful. Roach joined *Coin World* in 2006 as a columnist; he has served as associate editor and editor-in-chief, and currently is the publication's editor-at-large.

ABOUT THE AUTHOR

John M. Mercanti is an American sculptor and engraver, best known to numismatists as the 12th chief engraver of the U.S. Mint and the designer of many circulating and commemorative coins and medals. He created the reverse design of the American Silver Eagle bullion coin.

Mercanti was born in Philadelphia. It was there that he received his artistic training, at the Pennsylvania Academy of Fine Arts, the Philadelphia College of Art, and the Fleisher Art Memorial School. He began his career as an illustrator and in 1974 joined the U.S. Mint as a sculptor-engraver under the legendary Frank Gasparro. In 2006 Mercanti was named chief engraver (supervisor of design and master tooling development specialist), a position he held until his retirement in late 2010.

John Mercanti has produced more coin and medal designs than any other employee in the history of the U.S. Mint. Among his works (in addition to the American Silver Eagle) are gold and silver commemorative coins honoring the Statue of Liberty, the Olympic Games, Dwight Eisenhower, the Smithsonian Institution, and other important people, places, and events from American history; more than a dozen Congressional Gold Medals; five circulating State quarters; and numerous commemorative and bullion medals.

Mercanti resides in New Jersey, across the Delaware River not far from his workplace of nearly 40 years, the Philadelphia Mint.

Michael Reagan

FOREWORD

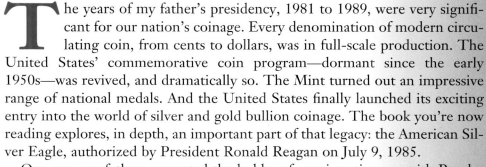

The years of my father's presidency, 1981 to 1989, were very significant for our nation's coinage. Every denomination of modern circulating coin, from cents to dollars, was in full-scale production. The United States' commemorative coin program—dormant since the early 1950s—was revived, and dramatically so. The Mint turned out an impressive range of national medals. And the United States finally launched its exciting entry into the world of silver and gold bullion coinage. The book you're now reading explores, in depth, an important part of that legacy: the American Silver Eagle, authorized by President Ronald Reagan on July 9, 1985.

One way my father supported the hobby of numismatics was with Proclamation 5027, signed by him on March 7, 1983, and filed with the Office of the Federal Register the following morning. With this he proclaimed the week beginning April 17, 1983, as being National Coin Week. "Since the beginning of history," he noted, "coins have played an important role in the story of civilization. They reflect the economic development of their country of origin, as well as the scientific advancement and artistic values of the people who produce and use them. Today, millions of Americans collect coins for both pleasure and profit."

In the text of the proclamation he remarked on the U.S. Mint's annual Proof sets, the new George Washington commemorative half dollar, and the upcoming (1983–1984) Los Angeles Olympiad coins ("the first commemorative Olympic coinage ever issued by our country will be introduced in gold and silver").

Furthermore, he recognized that "coin collecting has educational and cultural value, promotes greater understanding of our history and heritage, and is enjoyed by millions of Americans."

His signature sealed the proclamation: "Now, Therefore, I, Ronald Reagan, President of the United States of America, do hereby proclaim the week beginning April 17, 1983, as 'National Coin Week' and call upon the people of the United States to observe this week with appropriate ceremonies and activities."

Just over two years later, the president's signature would bring another boost to the hobby community. The Statue of Liberty–Ellis Island Commemorative Coin Act inaugurated the hugely popular 1986 half dollar, silver dollar, and gold $5 coins honoring the centennial of these national treasures. And an amendment to that bill—the Liberty Coin Act—was the start of the American Silver Eagle bullion program.

In this book, John Mercanti gives us a unique behind-the-scenes look at the design, production, and other creative and technical aspects of the American Silver Eagle. Mercanti knows what he's talking about—he's the talented sculptor-engraver who created the coin's reverse and helped render the redesign of Adolph Weinman's famous "Walking Liberty" obverse. His coauthor is Michael "Miles" Standish, one of the foremost experts on modern American coinage and a tireless promoter of this great national hobby. Together, Mercanti and Standish offer the definitive story of the American Silver Eagle. Whether you collect these coins, invest in them, or simply enjoy their rare artistry, you will benefit from this book.

The coin that started in President Reagan's second term has passed its quarter-century milestone and shows no sign of slowing down. Every year Americans (and collectors and investors worldwide) buy tens of millions of American Silver Eagles, adding them to their retirement accounts, displaying them proudly in their coin collections, and giving them to friends and family as treasured gifts. There are many wonderful facets to my father's presidential legacy. As someone who appreciates our nation's coins—and the history, culture, and heritage they represent—I am glad to count the American Silver Eagle as one of his contributions.

Michael Reagan
Sherman Oaks, California

Michael Reagan, the eldest son of President Ronald Reagan, is an author, columnist, social commentator, political strategist, and humanitarian. His career has included nationwide radio syndication with an audience of more than five million listeners. A world-record setter in power-boat racing, Reagan has used that venue to raise money and awareness for charities and causes like the U.S. Olympic Team, the Cystic Fibrosis and Juvenile Diabetes foundations, and the Statue of Liberty Restoration Fund. His books include *On the Outside Looking In, The Common Sense of an Uncommon Man: The Wit, Wisdom and Eternal Optimism of Ronald Reagan*, and *Twice Adopted*. Reagan serves on the board of the John Douglas French Alzheimer's Foundation and is president of the Reagan Legacy Foundation. He and his wife live in California.

The first coin of the modern era of commemoratives was the 1982 George Washington half dollar, a silver coin honoring the 250th anniversary of the first president's birth.

PREFACE TO THE FIRST EDITION

The hobby and investment communities have been due for a definitive reference and history book on American Silver Eagles for more than 25 years. These hugely popular coins—a third of a billion have been sold since 1986—are collected by numismatists, stockpiled by investors, and treasured by silver buyers throughout the United States and around the world.

A quick glance at annual sales shows how the American Silver Eagle has become more and more popular in recent years. (These numbers are for regular bullion strikes only; collector formats account for even more coins.)

2007	9,028,036	2010	29,110,500
2008	20,583,000	2011	39,768,000
2009	30,459,000	2012	40,000,000-plus (est.)

From time to time collectors have shared their research, theories, and insight into American Silver Eagles in hobby magazines, newspaper articles, and online forums. But until now, there has been no encyclopedic book-length study made on our nation's cornerstone bullion program. In *American Silver Eagles*, no less an expert than John M. Mercanti—12th chief engraver of the U.S. Mint, and the designer of the coin's reverse—shares his unique insight and perspective on these beautiful pieces of Americana.

This book is an overview for the newcomer to the series—the collector who wants a detailed but engagingly readable education in history, rarity levels, popular varieties, and market values. It's also a book for the longtime collector who wants a single-source reference: a guide not to be read once and then shelved, but to be kept handy for frequent visits and consultations. It's a textbook for the serious numismatist who wants an insider's view of the intricacies of design, engraving, production, and other technical and artistic factors. And for the investor this book introduces and explains the aspects and lure of numismatics—the art and science of the hobby of collecting coins—adding another aspect to the desirability of these interesting bullion issues.

To create this book, John Mercanti has drawn on nearly 40 years of experience working in the U.S. Mint, starting in 1974 as a sculptor-engraver and culminating with his 2006 appointment as chief engraver (supervisor of design and master tooling development specialist), a position he held until his retirement in late 2010. Trained at the Pennsylvania Academy of Fine Arts, the Philadelphia College of Art, and the Fleisher Art Memorial School, Mercanti produced more coin and medal designs than any other employee in the history of the U.S. Mint. As chief engraver, he was singularly positioned to observe and direct many of the Mint's operations, including those involving the American Silver Eagle bullion program. His firsthand knowledge and experience—both broad and deep—make him the perfect author for *American Silver Eagles*.

Mercanti was joined in production of this book by Michael "Miles" Standish, vice president and senior grader of the Professional Coin Grading Service (PCGS). A former authenticator for the American Numismatic Association and a 2011 recipient of the U.S. Mint Director's Coin for Excellence award, Standish has studied and/or graded the finest, rarest, and most valuable coins in the world. He brought to this project knowledge of the rare-coin market that comes only from long involvement and, having personally graded more than one million coins, extensive first-hand experience.

A foreword by social commentator Michael Reagan—eldest son of Ronald Reagan, under whose presidency the American Silver Eagle was launched—presents the book and its distinguished authors. Chapter 1 discusses the "why and how" of the United States' entrance into the modern bullion market. Chapter 2 is John Mercanti's behind-the-scenes history of the American Silver Eagle, its design development, the Mint's transition into digital design, and other elements of the coinage series. Chapter 3 presents a detailed date-by-date study of each American Silver Eagle, plus varieties and sets, with high-resolution photographs, rarity information, values, certified-coin populations, surface and strike characteristics, market details, and more. In chapter 4, you get an illustrated overview of other coins in our nation's bullion program, setting the American Silver Eagle in the context of a larger constellation of silver, gold, platinum, and palladium coins. Appendix charts compile the book's data in convenient format for easy coin-by-coin comparisons; an illustrated catalog presents the greater body of Mercanti's numismatic design work; a glossary of terms offers guidance to the beginning and intermediate collector and a refresher for the advanced numismatist; and the index provides a convenient and detailed resource for looking up the book's information.

These diverse elements—technical and artistic, historical and current, market-driven and hobbyist—combine to make *American Silver Eagles* a valuable addition to any collector's or investor's bookshelf.

PREFACE TO THE SECOND EDITION

If any numismatic book has earned the title of "runaway best-seller," it's *American Silver Eagles: A Guide to the U.S. Bullion Coin Program*. The first edition sold out in a few months, with tens of thousands of copies eagerly snapped up by enthusiastic coin collectors and investors. Author John Mercanti and Miles Standish promoted the book through social media and appearances including at the Whitman Coin & Collectibles Expo in Baltimore. *American Silver Eagles* quickly earned praise from the hobby community, with reviewers calling it "invaluable," "impressive," and "a book that belongs in your library"[1] . . . "a real pleasure to read, especially because of the lavish illustrations and the coffee-table format"[2] . . . "beautiful" and "vitally informative"[3] . . . "three books in one"[4] . . . "an outstanding reference" and "a great value"[5] . . . and a "comprehensive guide to [the] silver bullion coin" with "possibly everything you ever wanted to know about the silver American Eagle."[6]

In this, the second edition, the story of the American Silver Eagle is expanded to include new information on the U.S. Mint's individual coins and sets of 2012 and 2013. Additional research and more photographs expand the coverage of earlier issues, as well. More historical photographs have been added to the text. Certified coin populations are updated, as are the valuations seen in today's sometimes volatile marketplace. Additional images and information bring the book up to date in chapter 4 (covering the Mint's other silver, gold, and platinum issues, plus news on the Treasury's report on palladium coins). And a new appendix explores the phenomenon of surface spotting on American Silver Eagles.

These additions and updates, building on the solid foundation of the first edition, make *American Silver Eagles*, second edition, an equally valuable reference for every collector's and investor's library.

PREFACE TO THE THIRD EDITION

With its first two editions *American Silver Eagles* established itself as the standard reference on the U.S. Mint's biggest silver bullion coin program. In the short period since the publication of the second edition in 2013, collectors and investors have purchased many tens of millions more of the coins. The program's record-setting 2014 bullion-coin mintage exceeded 44 million ounces. Strong demand continued, and in 2015 even that massive quantity was overtaken, before the end of November. Stacked on top of the bullion, the Mint's Burnished and Proof numismatic collectible versions add millions more to the mintages of these beautiful and historic coins.

In the third edition of *American Silver Eagles* you'll find updated market information including population data for professionally graded and certified coins; retail values in multiple grades; and analysis of activity in the secondary market. The coin-by-coin catalog has been updated to include the bullion-strike and numismatic issues of 2014 and 2015. Mintages have been revised for recent productions to reflect the latest U.S. Mint audits. The illustrated catalog of John Mercanti's numismatic work has been expanded to showcase even more of his creativity. And a new illustrated check-list and record-keeping appendix provides a handy way to keep track of your coin collection.

The American Silver Eagles continue to soar to new heights. John Mercanti's guide remains the collector's and investor's best field book for these popular and uniquely American coins.

On July 9, 1985, President Ronald Reagan signed the Liberty
Coin Act, which gave birth to the American Silver Eagle.

1

History of the U.S. Bullion Coin Program

The American Silver Eagle bullion program was launched in the 1980s. Its debut was influenced by numerous factors on the national and world scenes. In many ways, however, the stage had been set 50 years earlier, during the Great Depression.

From the mid-1930s to the mid-1960s, the value of gold was pegged by the U.S. government at a steady $35 an ounce. Silver, meanwhile, fluctuated between roughly $0.30 and $0.90 an ounce up to the early 1960s.

In 1933 President Franklin Roosevelt signed Executive Order 6102, forbidding the hoarding of gold. The order required "all persons" to "deliver on or before May 1, 1933 all gold coin, gold bullion, and Gold Certificates now owned by them to a Federal Reserve Bank, branch or agency, or to any member bank of the Federal Reserve System." Criminal penalties for violation of the order were a fine of up to $10,000 or jail time of up to 10 years—or both. (Exceptions were made for reasonable amounts of gold used in industry, professions like dentistry, and the arts; rare coins owned by collectors; and a few other special cases. Also, individuals could hold small amounts of gold coinage—up to $100 but no more.) The president's order was designed to protect the nation's banking system, which was fragile and wounded in the early years of the Great Depression.

As instructed, Americans turned in millions of gold coins. These were melted and eventually stored as bars at the United States Bullion Depository, Fort Knox. The value of the gold held by the Federal Reserve tripled between 1933 and 1937.

In 1933, President Franklin Roosevelt signed an executive order prohibiting the hoarding of gold. The ban would stand until 1975.

It was the Gold Reserve Act of 1934 that changed the dollar value of gold from $20.67 to $35 per ounce. This official government price remained in effect until August 15, 1971, when President Richard Nixon announced that the United States would no longer convert dollars to gold at a fixed value. With that, the country was off the gold standard (which it had been on officially since 1900, and de facto for decades before that).

In 1974 Congress and President Gerald Ford re-legalized the private ownership of gold coins, bars, and certificates, effective December 31. After more than 40 years, Americans could once again legally own as much gold as they wanted.

Millions of U.S. gold coins were turned in to the Federal Reserve following Executive Order 6102. (shown enlarged)

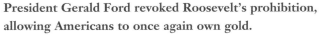

President Gerald Ford revoked Roosevelt's prohibition, allowing Americans to once again own gold.

INTERNATIONAL COMPETITION IN GOLD

A few years after President Ford's 1974 executive order revoked the ban on gold, the United States would begin offering silver, gold, and platinum coins for sale to collectors and investors. Before that, however, several other nations (notably South Africa, Canada, China, Mexico, and Australia) were minting their own gold bullion coins.

South Africa's Krugerrand was first struck in 1967; it proved very popular and by 1980 had captured 90% of the world's gold-coin market. (In the United States, importing Krugerrands was illegal starting in 1985. This was an economic sanction against the South African government, to punish and discourage its racial-segregation policies. The sanction was lifted in 1994 when South Africa officially abandoned apartheid.)

The Krugerrand's success encouraged other gold-producing countries to develop their own bullion programs. Canada launched the gold Maple Leaf in 1979. Mexico, with a long tradition of minting gold and silver coins, authorized its Libertad in 1981. China's Panda series began in 1982. Australia introduced its gold Nugget in 1986, and the United Kingdom debuted the Britannia in 1987. Austria began its Vienna Philharmonic gold-coin program in 1989, and it quickly became a best-seller. All of these coins, as well as the Krugerrand, had official legal-tender status backed by their issuing governments.

Other gold-producing nations saw the success of South Africa's Krugerrand starting in the 1960s, and were inspired to introduce their own bullion coins. The United States would eventually enter the market.

Starting in 1980, the United States attempted to compete with these international products and capture some of the market in gold. The congressionally mandated vehicle was the "American Arts Commemorative Series" of gold medals. Unlike the Krugerrand and other international coins, these medals were not legal tender—in fact, they were at first designed specifically not to resemble traditional U.S. coinage. Sales were slow from the start; the marketing was clumsy, and buyers were confronted by constantly changing prices based on daily bullion values. Even a rejuvenated marketing effort in 1982 failed to boost the program. It sputtered out and ended in 1984. (For more about these medals, see chapter 4. They are also explored in detail in *American Gold and Silver: U.S. Mint Collector and Investor Coins and Medals, Bicentennial to Date*, by Dennis Tucker.)

In December 1985, the Gold Bullion Coin Act of 1985 finally established a truly competitive American product, with full legal-tender status—the American Gold Eagle. Meanwhile, on the silver scene, events had been set in motion that would bring about an equally historic coin.

The United States' first post–Executive Order 6102 entry into the gold market was the American Arts Commemorative Series. Its half-ounce and one-ounce medals honored Willa Cather, Mark Twain, and other American writers, artists, and musicians.

The U.S. Mint's bullion coinage program has grown to include silver, gold, and platinum in various formats, with palladium scheduled for possible production. The Mint defines a bullion coin thus: "A bullion coin is a coin that is valued by its weight in a specific precious metal. Unlike commemorative or numismatic coins valued by limited mintage, rarity, condition and age, bullion coins are purchased by investors seeking a simple and tangible means to own and invest in the gold, silver, and platinum markets."

THE DOMESTIC SITUATION IN SILVER

In the 1970s and early 1980s, executive plans were afoot to sell off precious metal from the Defense National Stockpile Center (a branch of the federal Defense Logistics Agency, whose purpose is to store, secure, and sell raw materials). Several presidential administrations were convinced that domestic production of silver was far greater than any strategic need for the metal, and sought—mostly unsuccessfully—to liquidate part of the nation's stockpile. Powerful forces in the mining states resisted such selloffs, fearing that they would flood the market with silver and decrease its value. (A September 1976 *Wall Street Journal* article noted that "When the US government makes noises about selling silver from the federal stockpile, futures traders start unloading futures contracts in speculation that such a sale would depress prices."[1]) Certain military-minded lawmakers also opposed the sale of stockpiled silver, wanting guarantees that the proceeds would be used not simply to reduce the federal debt, but to buy other materials needed for national defense.

A sampling of *Wall Street Journal* headlines from the era illustrates the challenges various presidents faced in selling off the stockpiled silver:

> "Nixon Plan to Sell Stockpiled Commodities Could Be Slowed by Market, Legal Snags," March 16, 1973

> "House Committee Rejects Sales of Silver from Government's Strategic Stockpile," September 12, 1979

> "House Refuses to Sell Any Silver in U.S. Stockpile: Compromise That Called for Sale of 5 Million Ounces Loses by Lopsided Margin," December 13, 1979

> "House Panel Rejects Reagan Bid to Sell All of Silver in Stockpile," June 5, 1981

For more than 170 years, many U.S. coins, like the half dollar seen here, were made of .900 fine silver. By the 1960s the precious metal was too expensive to use for coinage, and the Mint introduced a new composition of copper and nickel. Still, Uncle Sam held massive reserves of silver as part of the national-defense stockpile.

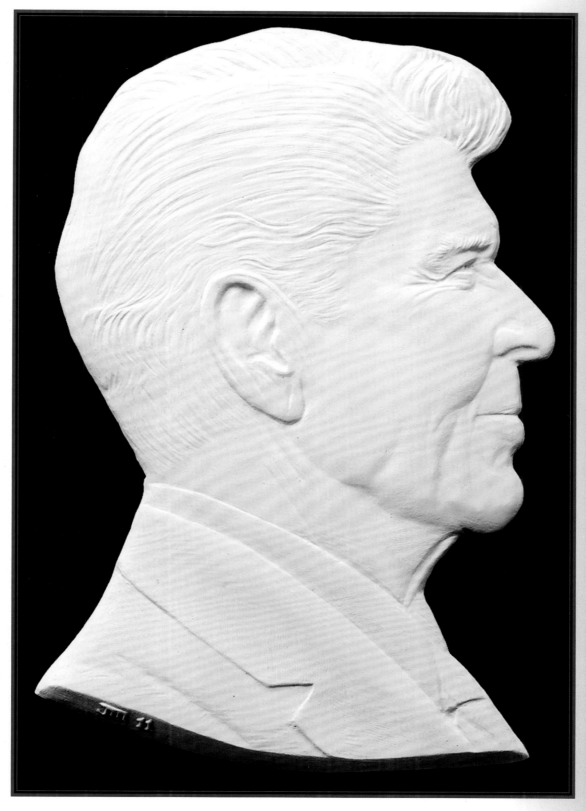

President Ronald Reagan, as well as several of his predecessors, sought to sell off part or all of the nation's stockpile of silver, arguing that domestic production exceeded the amount needed for strategic purposes. (Bas-relief sculpture by John M. Mercanti.)

Senator James McClure of Idaho sought to protect his state's mining interests—in particular, keeping the price of silver as high as possible. McClure was the influential chairman of the Senate Energy and Natural Resources Committee. Toward the end of his political career, he was described by Senator Malcolm Wallop of Wyoming: "There is no major piece of energy, public lands, or natural resources legislation passed in recent years on which he has not left an imprint."[2]

President Ronald Reagan.

Despite such opposition, the government did sell portions of its silver. On June 10, 1981, the House Armed Services Committee decided to approve the Reagan administration's request to sell federal silver, beginning in fiscal year 1982, to help balance the budget. The next month, Congress agreed to allow the sale of three-quarters of the stockpiled silver—105.1 million troy ounces—over a three-year period. When news got out, investors balked, and that September the market value of silver fell 11 percent. (Gold prices also dropped.) A group of politicians from Idaho, a major silver-mining state, tried to block the silver sales, the first of which was held in October 1981. On December 3, they proposed an amendment to the 1982 Department of Defense appropriation bill to end the federal sale of silver "until the President, not later than July 1, 1982, redetermines that the silver authorized for disposal is excess to the requirements of the stockpile." When the appropriations bill was signed into law with the amendment still attached, further sales of the silver were effectively blocked.

On May 27, 1982, Senator James McClure and Representative Larry Craig (both of Idaho) introduced identical bills in the Senate and House "to provide for the disposal of silver from the National Defense Stockpile through the issuance of silver coins." Their thinking appears to have been, "We can't fight the silver selloff forever; if it has to occur, at least we can try to control it." Presumably the sale of, say, 10 million ounces of silver coins to hundreds of thousands of Americans would depress the price of silver less than the same weight sold in bulk to a few large wholesale buyers. The bills' stated objectives were to "redirect the sale of silver from our national defense stockpile in an effort to minimize its [effect] on the already depressed price of silver."

The bills were both referred to committee and never enacted.

That June the price of silver soared when Secretary of the Interior James Watt announced that the federal sale of stockpiled silver would be indefinitely postponed. (The government's mandated study on potential methods of selling the silver had been delayed.)

On January 27, 1983, Senator McClure introduced another bill that was nearly identical to the May 1982 proposal. "If we are forced to accept a sale," McClure asked, "why use the method guaranteed to depress the price and dispose of the silver with the lowest possible return to the taxpayers? Why not instead, if we must sell, at least get as much for it as we can?" His solution: "legislation which provides that in the event the President proposes and Congress authorizes the sale of silver from the strategic stockpile, this silver would be sold through the minting and distribution of a silver-bearing coin."[3] Like the 1982 bill, this one was referred to committee; hearings were held, but it was not enacted.

Sales of the silver remained suspended for more than two years. Finally, Senator McClure on June 21, 1985, proposed the Liberty Coin Act—an amendment to the Statue of Liberty–Ellis Island Commemorative Coin Act, then being considered in the House of Representatives. The Senate agreed to the amendment, the House approved the amended bill, and on July 9 President Ronald Reagan signed it into law.

Remember Your First Thrill of AMERICAN LIBERTY

The authorization for a new bullion coinage program in 1986 was tacked on to the law that authorized these Statue of Liberty coins, part of the United States' commemorative coin program. Mint engraver John Mercanti designed the Statue of Liberty silver dollar as well as the reverse of the American Silver Eagle.

The Liberty Coin Act:

- authorized the secretary of the Treasury to mint and issue silver bullion coins
- specified the diameter, weight, fineness, general design, inscriptions, and edge format of the coins
- established the formula for pricing the coins
- defined the coins as having both numismatic and legal-tender status
- specified that the silver would come from the national stockpiles
- set the act in effect as of October 1, 1985
- stipulated that no coins would be issued or sold before September 1, 1986

Secretary of the Treasury James Baker presided over the striking of the first American Silver Eagle on October 29, 1986, in a special ceremony in San Francisco (at the U.S. Mint's Assay Office). As Baker "reached for the electronic button on press No. 105, he turned to the audience and said, 'I don't need a pick and shovel to start the San Francisco Silver Rush of 1986.'"[4]

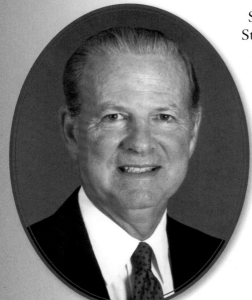

Secretary Baker's analogy to an old-time gold rush was apt. The United States' bullion program started quietly but over the years has grown into a case of "silver fever." Between the bullion coins and various collectible formats, more than 400 million ounces have been sold since 1986. The coins are readily available in the numismatic marketplace, and also from banks, investment firms, and other mainstream channels. In the 30 years since the American Silver Eagle was launched, the coin has become one of the most popular silver-investment vehicles in the world.

James Baker was secretary of the Treasury when the American Silver Eagle program began.

The American Silver Eagle (face value $1, actual silver weight one ounce) is a legal-tender bullion coin with weight, content, and purity guaranteed by the United States government. It is one of very few silver coins allowed in individual retirement accounts (IRAs). The obverse features Adolph A. Weinman's Liberty Walking design, as used on the circulating half dollar of 1916 to 1947. The reverse design, by John Mercanti, is a rendition of a heraldic eagle.

2
Behind the Scenes at the U.S. Mint

I've often been asked, "What is the coin design process like? How do you design a coin? Who selects the final design?" So let's take some time to explore that aspect of the coining process, along with some of my personal experiences, with special emphasis on the American Silver Eagle.

MY BREAKTHROUGH INTO ENGRAVING

There were five engravers plus the chief engraver on staff when I came to the Mint in 1974. At the time Frank Gasparro had been chief engraver for a number of years. He had been appointed to the position on February 23, 1965, and would hold it until his retirement on January 16, 1981.

Toward the end of 1973 I had been working as an illustrator for a federal agency that supported all the military services—Army, Navy, Air Force, Marines, and Coast Guard. I had been with the federal government almost six years. I was married, with an infant son, working three jobs to make ends meet, and I wasn't happy with the position I held at the time because I saw no future advancement.

One afternoon I was reviewing competitive open positions within the federal government. I saw that there was an opening for an apprentice at the United States Mint, and I decided to apply.

I filled out the required paperwork and waited.

I was called a few weeks later and was told that I would be interviewed by Mr. Gasparro who was the chief engraver and that I should call him for an appointment.

I immediately called to set up a meeting date. Frank was cordial and asked me if I had ever done anything related to medallic art.

"Most of my training to date has been in drawing and illustrating," I replied. He told me that was great, because a large amount of time would be spent on the board creating designs. He also requested I model something in relief and bring it to him—in two days.

Needless to say, panic alarms went off all around me. What would I do?

I immediately went to my library and opened a coffee-table book on Michelangelo. I sketched one of the prophets from the painting on the Sistine Chapel ceiling (Zechariah, to be exact). Now all I had to do was model it in clay. Piece of cake!

I happened to have on hand in my workshop a piece of wood about seven inches in diameter. I gessoed it white (gesso is a paint mixture, a binder com-

U.S. MINT CHIEF ENGRAVER
FRANK GASPARRO

Frank Gasparro was born August 26, 1909, in Philadelphia. His father was a musician and wanted his son to follow in his footsteps, but young Frank had another calling: the visual arts. He apprenticed under sculptor Giuseppe Donato, who had worked for the legendary Auguste Rodin. After studying at the Fleisher Art Memorial school and the Pennsylvania Academy of Fine Arts, he won two scholarships and continued to learn and practice his craft in France, Italy, Germany, England, and Sweden.

Starting in 1937 Gasparro worked as a sculptor for the Federal Arts Administration. He joined the Philadelphia Mint in December 1942, working under Chief Engraver John R. Sinnock (who later would design the Roosevelt dime and the Franklin half dollar, among other coins), and then under Chief Engraver Gilroy Roberts (who designed the obverse of the Kennedy half dollar). His projects included various medals, and coins struck for other countries.

In 1959 Assistant Engraver Gasparro's first major U.S. coinage design debuted: a new reverse for the Lincoln cent. The coin, like Gasparro, had been born in 1909, a hundred years after the birth of Abraham Lincoln, and in its 50th year its famous "wheat ears" reverse was replaced by Gasparro's rendition of the Lincoln Memorial. His design entry was chosen from among 23 reviewed at the Mint.

He created the reverse of the John F. Kennedy half dollar after the president was martyred in late 1963.

Gasparro was appointed chief engraver in 1965. Among his later coinage designs are the Eisenhower and Susan B. Anthony dollars. He created medals honoring Winston Churchill, Douglas MacArthur, John Wayne, and other famous people, and also the presidential medals for every chief executive from Lyndon Johnson to Ronald Reagan.

bined with chalk, gypsum, or pigment). Then I transferred the drawing onto it and began building up the clay portrait.

I've heard of people having epiphanies in their lives where an event or experience changed them forever. I never thought I would ever have such an experience. I loved illustrating, I had learned from the best, and I knew I would spend the rest of my life creating images on paper. But when I began modeling that one portrait and the image began to take shape, I knew there was no going back. I had to have this job. At that point I wanted nothing else but to be a medallic sculptor.

I still have that portrait and it's still in clay. I've never cast it.

I finished the portrait as best I could, packed it up with my portfolio, and kept my appointment with Frank.

JOINING THE U.S. MINT

Frank Gasparro was always a hard person to read. Serious, but never angry. At that first meeting, as I showed him my work, all he said was, "Very nice, very nice, yes, yes, very nice." That's it. That's all he said. Never introduced me to the staff or showed me around the department. He politely asked if I had any questions. He answered them, and said he'd call me and let me know about the position. Then he sent me on my way.

I left not knowing what kind of impression I'd made.

The sculpture of Zechariah that John Mercanti modeled for his interview at the U.S. Mint.

After 15 years as chief engraver, Frank Gasparro retired from the U.S. Mint, in January 1981. He continued to design medals for private and public groups, and also taught at the Fleisher Art Memorial, where he had studied in his youth. He was 92 years old when he passed away on September 29, 2001.

"More than any other chief engraver up to that time," writes Q. David Bowers in the *Guide Book of Lincoln Cents*, "Gasparro was a warm, friendly, outgoing man who loved numismatics and enjoyed meeting members of the coin collecting community."[1]

In his obituary, the *New York Times* noted: "His daughter said her father, a slight man with a Jimmy Durante profile, had strong, large hands and liked to work in alabaster. When he introduced himself to strangers as a sculptor, he had a ready reply when they asked where they might find his work. 'It's in your pocket,' he said."[2] His artistry was coined on more than 100 billion Lincoln cents.

A month went by and I hadn't heard anything from the Mint so I decided to call and check the status of the position. That call was a life changer. Human Resources told me that Frank had selected me for the apprenticeship and that they'd been trying to reach me for a week, but they must have had the wrong contact number.

And that's it—that's how I got the position.

I'll always be grateful to Frank for hiring me. He was a great teacher and a great friend. I have many, many funny stories about him, including those he told me about himself. A few weeks after he retired in 1981 I met him for lunch. I took along a tape recorder and he told me all the stories about his life and career related to the Mint, and stories of his early life. But that's for another time and another book.

John Mercanti: first week on the job as a sculptor-engraver at the U.S. Mint, 1974.

THE MINT'S ENGRAVERS AND DESIGNERS

At the time I came on board at the U.S. Mint, in 1974, there were five engravers on staff.

There was Edgar Z. Steever—a brilliant mind—who had two parents who were physicians, and could have been one himself.

Michael G. Iacocca, who was one of the best portrait artists I ever met.

Sherl Joseph Winter, an incredible portraitist and numismatic sculptor and designer, who taught me so much.

John Mercanti, circa 1975, about one year into his long career at the Philadelphia Mint.

Philip J. Fowler, who was, for want of a better word, one of the great "characters" in my early career, introducing me to the arts, music, and some of the finest wine and cuisine in Philadelphia and New York.

And finally, Matthew Peloso, who came to the Mint soon after I arrived. Matt was the biggest man I had ever met, well over six feet tall, with hands that dwarfed everyone else's, but when he picked up a tool he could sculpt the finest detail. He had the touch of an angel.

These men were so instrumental to me in my early career that no story of me and my accomplishments is complete without them. Some never had a design selected for a circulating coin, but nonetheless they are a vital part of numismatic history.

Many years later, in 2003, the Mint would launch its Artistic Infusion Program. The program is composed of two categories of artists: master designers and associate designers. At the start of the program there was another category, for student artists, but it was discontinued a few years later.

The purpose of the program is to add to the Mint's design portfolio artists with unique and varied disciplines such as illustrating, painting, and sculpture. As of this writing it has proven to be highly successful, and from the program have emerged some of the best designers in the country.

The design process evolved into an in-house competition that still exists today. There were times, but very infrequently, when an engraver would be assigned to develop a design for a specific program. I, as chief engraver, did at times delegate a specific engraver to work on an obverse or reverse design, or a particular program, especially if I felt his or her talents and strengths lent themselves to that project.

In the past, under the auspices of Frank Gasparro and chief engravers before him, it was extremely hard for a staff engraver to have his design selected for any coin. (I say *his* because in those days the staff was all male.) The chief engraver had first pick at every program. That was just the way the system ran: it was a hierarchy, with the chief engraver at the top. You either accepted it or you moved on—and yes, there were a few engravers who were very unhappy with the situation, and moved on very quickly. If the staff were lucky, they might be assigned a reverse design. This is a fact that is easily documented by checking the Mint medal catalog. The majority of significant programs were designed and sculpted by chief engravers.

I particularly remember designing for the J. Edgar Hoover medal. Frank Gasparro called a staff meeting advising us that he was designing and sculpting

A gathering of Mint staff celebrating Frank Gasparro's 70th birthday, August 1979. All of the Philadelphia Mint's engravers are present. Gasparro is standing fourth from the left, in jacket and tie. Matthew Peloso is second from the left; Michael Iacocco stands behind him. Sherl Winter is the mustachioed man in the back, center. In the necktie, directly above the portrait of John Wayne, is Philip Fowler; in the back, behind him, is Edgar Steever. John Mercanti stands at far right.

the obverse and that we, the staff, would be graced by being allowed to submit reverse designs. (The Hoover reverse was the first of my designs selected for a production medal.) This was the same procedure Gasparro used for presidential medals.

This system ultimately began evolving into something different. In time it was requested that engravers submit designs for both obverses and reverses of coins and medal programs. We were generally allotted two weeks to submit several obverse designs and another two weeks for reverse designs. I'm not sure what precipitated this change, but I feel the Mint wanted to begin using the diversity of its in-house talent. In my early years with the Mint, the mid-1970s and early '80s, I had the privilege of working with some of the most talented sculptors and numismatic artists in the country, and it was great to see that they were getting a chance to display their talents.

Frank Gasparro autographing a photo of his Susan B. Anthony dollar design at the coin's launch, February 2, 1979.

DESIGNING A COIN OR MEDAL

There are many factors related to design that go into the production of a coin or medal. As examples: The relationship of elements working in harmony with each other. The attitude of the subject or main element. Is the figure looking in the right direction? Is the pose conveying the necessary message? Or the flow of the text: Does the text intersect or overlap the main or secondary elements? Will the text run over or under, around or through, any of the elements?

The sum of all these factors is what makes an artistically pleasing design and, ultimately, sculpture.

In my experience there are designers, good designers, and great designers. I've worked with them all. Some would answer the design questions and meet

John Mercanti working on the reverse of the J. Edgar Hoover medal, around 1975.

the criteria above and consider the final product adequate. Others had and still have a certain passion in them—that passion that prohibits satisfaction with a product until the day of the deadline is upon them and designs are due. They constantly tweak, searching for perfection.

Any form of art is a lifestyle. You can't leave it after eight or ten hours. It stays with you, it is you and who you are. You're a painter, a sculptor, a designer, a potter. Whatever form of art you practice, you live it and breathe it. It's who you are as a person. It's your identity.

I've had members of my staff tell me that an idea for a particular program came to them in the shower, or that in the middle of the night they had a dream with a design resolution. It's a passion and a fire in your soul that's never extinguished.

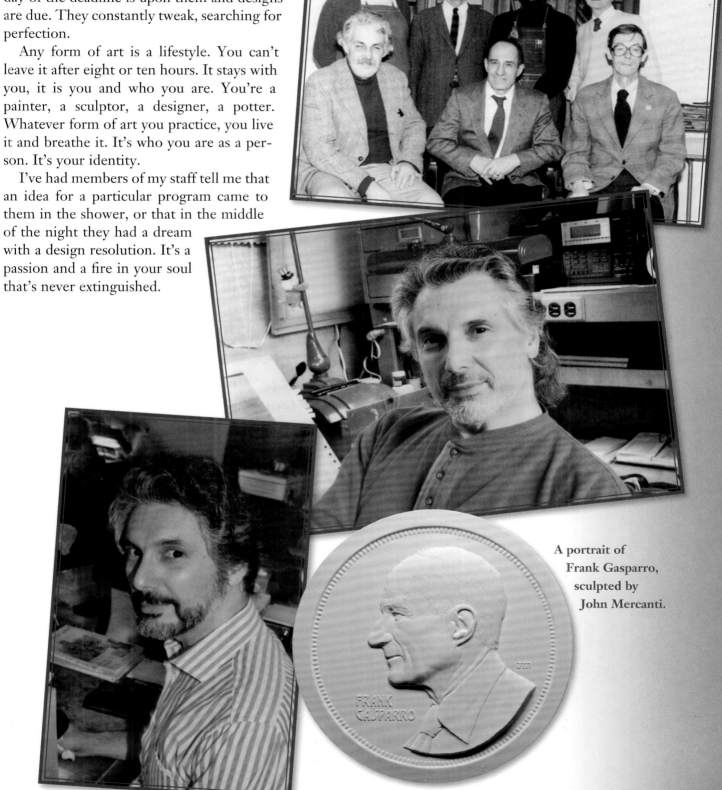

A portrait of
Frank Gasparro,
sculpted by
John Mercanti.

FRANK GASPARRO

ELEMENTS OF GOOD DESIGN

The following are a few examples of what I consider good coin and medal designs. I have not included any of my own work in these examples. Please understand that these are my personal opinions based on 40-plus years of work in the industry, and might not reflect the opinions of numismatic writers and scholars. They may completely disagree with me; I'm okay with that. Let's get started:

The Liberty Cap half cent coins of 1793 and 1794 to me are the perfect example of Primitive American Folk Art. They beautifully display simplicity and balance. The artwork on the obverse and reverse is simply rendered with no extraneous detail and is a delight to behold.

The original 1913 Buffalo nickel. Most people don't know that the original artwork is only a little over four inches in diameter. The coin is perfectly designed to scale. The size of the portrait and the buffalo beautifully fill the basin, and the design is instantly readable. It's the perfect coin.

The Little Rock Central High School Desegregation commemorative obverse. This coin was designed by Richard Masters, who worked with me as an AIP (Artistic Infusion Program) designer. When Rick first submitted his initial drafts they were completely different from the winning design. There were full figures, with readable faces. We didn't want to be person-specific; the figures had to be generic. After a few rounds I suggested that Rick submit a draft showing figures from the waist down only. He did, and the final design eventually evolved. This coin received a COTY (Coin of the Year) award and I'm extremely proud of what Rick accomplished.

1999 George Washington Death Bicentennial $5 gold commemorative, by Laura Gardin Fraser. This design, to me, should have been the 1932 quarter dollar. It won the competition but it was deemed unworthy because it was designed by a woman. It is, in my opinion, far superior to the selected design submitted by John Flanagan. Fraser's is a far better rendered portrait. It's more powerful and fills the basin better. Her reverse is more heraldic and powerful. Flanagan's eagle has no strength and resembles a pigeon. The injustice that her design was not selected irritates me to this day.

The Congressional Gold Medal commemorating the Dalai Lama. The obverse is a beautiful portrait designed and rendered by Don Everhart. Don was my second in command and could model a portrait faster than anyone I ever knew. He is also one of the premier medallic artists in the industry. This is a wonderfully balanced piece. The simplicity of the reverse perfectly reflects the simple life of the Dalai Lama. It was rendered by staff sculptor Joseph Menna.

The commemorative gold medal honoring Women Airforce Service Pilots (WASP). The obverse was designed by Joel Iskowitz (of the Artistic Infusion Program) and rendered by Mint staff sculptor Phebe Hemphill. Since being selected as an AIP designer, Joel has evolved into one of the best designers in the program. He has had many designs selected for coins and medals and I'm happy to have had the privilege of working with him. Phebe's execution of the clay model, the sensitivity in the way she's rendered the portrait and the figures, is breathtakingly beautiful. As far as low-relief sculpture goes, Phebe is the 21st-century John Sinnock. There's no one better. Once I saw Phebe's work I knew immediately I wanted her on the Mint's staff. I stole her from McFarlane Toys, where she was a staff sculptor, and to this day have no regrets about it. Don Everhart's perfectly balanced reverse design beautifully describes the story of the WASP fliers.

DESIGN SELECTION

Let's now turn to design selection.

Before 2003, when the Citizens Coinage Advisory Committee was formed, all designs were vetted in house at the Mint. Included in the evaluation process were representatives from sales and marketing and the legal department, the Mint director, and his or her associates.

Any form of design evaluation, be it in house or by committee, can be, for want of a better word, challenging. In my personal experience with committees, people are appointed to serve who generally don't have the full depth of experience to make a sound design decision, because they come from various backgrounds and occupations not related to the arts. Lawyers, doctors, accountants, coin collectors. They lack the eye and background of the designer—although that doesn't mean they don't have the passion to produce the best product possible. A great deal of diplomacy is required in officiating these meetings.

Once the designs were selected they would be forwarded to the U.S. Commission of Fine Arts in Washington. The CFA is a federal commission made up of representatives from various sectors of the arts. They're responsible for overseeing, evaluating, and approving everything in the federal government related to art and architecture. Nothing that has anything to do with the federal government (outside of some areas managed by the Architect of the Capitol) gets built, issued, sculpted, or painted unless it's first reviewed, modified, and finally approved by this committee. The Commission of Fine Arts is chaired by the best and brightest in the country.

Once all committee recommendations, modifications, and redraws were approved, modeling could begin.

With any coin or medal program, the process begins with legislation. The American Silver Eagle program was no exception. The law as written stated that the coin would have a design symbolic of Liberty on the obverse, and an

THE CITIZENS COINAGE ADVISORY COMMITTEE

The CCAC was established by Congress in 2003, under Public Law 108-15, to advise the secretary of the Treasury on the themes and designs of all U.S. coins and medals. This includes circulating coinage, commemoratives, bullion, Congressional gold medals, and national and other medals. The committee advises on the events, persons, and places to be honored by the issuance of commemorative coins, and makes recommendations with respect to their mintage levels. It serves as an informed, experienced, and impartial resource to the secretary of the Treasury and represents the interests of American citizens and coin collectors. CCAC meetings are public, and a letter of minutes is submitted to the secretary of the Treasury after each gathering. More information is available online at ccac.gov.

eagle on the reverse. Such instructions, as written in coinage laws, can be more or less ambiguous and not always well defined. This of course leaves many options for the designers in their interpretations of design elements.

The design process for the American Silver Eagle program began immediately after the staff completed designs for the Statue of Liberty–Ellis Island coins. As I think back, we may have worked on both programs simultaneously, since both were attached to the same legislation with the same issue date.

As fate would have it, my designs were selected for the Statue of Liberty–Ellis Island silver dollar obverse and reverse. This was an honor I never expected. My grandparents came to this country as immigrants from Sicily early in the 20th century, and it made me proud that I could honor them with this coin.

Not every coin design makes its way into final production, of course—not even if its artist is the Mint's chief engraver. Frank Gasparro's favorite design was his 1977 proposal for a small-diameter dollar coin, featuring a rendition of Miss Liberty. The design was not used because Congress mandated that the coin portray American civil-rights leader Susan B. Anthony. This bronzed plaster of Gasparro's Liberty is in the archives of the National Numismatic Collection in the Smithsonian Institution—a reminder of "what might have been."

THE U.S. COMMISSION OF FINE ARTS

The Commission of Fine Arts, established in 1910 by Act of Congress, is charged with giving expert advice to the president, Congress, and the heads of departments and agencies of the federal and District of Columbia governments on matters of design and aesthetics, "as they affect the federal interest and preserve the dignity of the nation's capital," per the Commission's official literature. The Commission consists of seven "well qualified judges of the fine arts" who are appointed by the president and serve for a term of four years; they may also be reappointed.

The Commission advises the U.S. Mint on the design of coins and medals, in accordance with the Commemorative Works Act. Its members review sketches such as the ones pictured here, developed for the Frances Cleveland $10 coin (part of the First Spouse gold bullion program).

THE LIBERTY COIN ACT

The Liberty Coin Act was tacked onto the 1985 legislation that authorized the Statue of Liberty commemorative coins. With this act, the American Silver Eagle was written into law.

Title II — LIBERTY COINS[3]

Sec. 201. Short Title.

This title may be cited as the "Liberty Coin Act."

Sec. 202. Minting of Silver Coins.

Section 5112 of title 31, United States Code, is amended by striking out subsections (e) and (f) and inserting in lieu thereof the following new subsections:

(e) Notwithstanding any other provision of law, the Secretary shall mint and issue, in quantities sufficient to meet public demand, coins which—

(1) are 40.6 millimeters in diameter and weigh 31.103 grams;

(2) contain .999 fine silver;

(3) have a design—

(A) symbolic of Liberty on the obverse side; and

(B) of an eagle on the reverse side;

(4) have inscriptions of the year of minting or issuance, and the words 'Liberty,' 'In God We Trust,' 'United States of America,' '1 Oz. Fine Silver,' 'E Pluribus Unum,' and 'One Dollar'; and

(5) have reeded edges.

(f) The Secretary shall sell the coins minted under subsection (e) to the public at a price equal to the market value of the bullion at the time of sale, plus the cost of minting, marketing, and distributing such coins (including labor, materials, dyes [sic], use of machinery, and overhead expenses).

(g) For purposes of section 5132(a)(1) of this title, all coins minted under subsection (e) of this section shall be considered to be numismatic items.

(h) The coins issued under this title shall be legal tender as provided in section 5103 of title 31, United States Code.

Sec. 203. Purchase of Silver.

Section 5116(b) of title 31, United States Code, is amended—

(1) in the first sentence of paragraph (1), by striking out "The Secretary shall" and inserting in lieu thereof "The Secretary may";

(2) by striking out the second sentence of paragraph (1); and

(3) by inserting after the first sentence of paragraph (2) the following new sentence: "The Secretary shall obtain the silver for the coins authorized under section 5112(e) of this title by purchase from stockpiles established under the Strategic and Critical Materials Stock Piling Act (50 U.S.C. 98 et seq.)."

Sec. 204. Conforming Amendment.

The third sentence of section 5132(a)(1) of title 31, United States Code, is amended by inserting "minted under section 5112(a) of this title" after "proof coins."

Sec. 205. Effective Date.

This title shall take effect on October 1, 1985, except that no coins may be issued or sold under subsection (e) of section 5112 of title 31, United States Code, before September 1, 1986, or before the date on which all coins minted under title I of this Act have been sold, whichever is earlier.

Approved July 9, 1985.

The Statue of Liberty commemorative silver dollar has special significance to the families of immigrants. John Mercanti's paternal grandparents (seen here on their wedding day) came to the United States in the early 1900s. Also pictured: his grandmother and mother.

DESIGN AND PREPARATION OF THE AMERICAN SILVER EAGLE OBVERSE AND REVERSE

Preparation of the Obverse

The obverse design of the American Silver Eagle was predetermined: it would be Adolph A. Weinman's Walking Liberty, originally issued on the half dollar in 1916 and in production until 1947. I have no idea who made that decision. It could have come from the Mint director, from sales and marketing, or from someone lobbying for it.

ADOLPH A. WEINMAN

Adolph Alexander Weinman was born in Karlsruhe, in the German grand duchy of Baden, on December 11, 1870. He came to the United States at the age of 10, and at 15 he attended evening classes at Cooper Union in Manhattan's East Village. Later he studied at the Art Students League of New York, under renowned sculptors Augustus Saint-Gaudens and Philip Martiny. The young artist served as an assistant to Charles Niehaus, Olin Warner, and Daniel Chester French before opening his own studio in 1904. Weinman was a talented and in-demand creator of architectural and monumental works, with many important large sculptures to his credit—but he is perhaps best known for his smaller-sized artistry on medals and coins. His personifications of American Liberty were minted on billions of silver dimes and half dollars from 1916 into the late 1940s.

Sculptors Adolph A. Weinman (front left) and Charles Keck (seated, front, in vest) pose with artists and a model, possibly at the Art Students League of New York, circa 1897.

What the average collector may not know but the numismatic scholar does is that the master plaster for the Weinman Walking Liberty obverse is only six inches in diameter. When you consider the amount of fine detail of the piece and the sculptural beauty of it, you appreciate the skill and knowledge required to achieve what Weinman did on such a scale. The final product is an absolute masterpiece.

There were some technical problems that had to be addressed. At that period in time, when a medallic sculptor modeled a coin in clay, the basin (a concave plaster model that the sculptor models the portraits, figures, text, or various other elements on) was made by hand. I know this because in my formative years at the Mint I was required to make them, in various sizes from three inches to twelve inches. The process was simple but not so easy. It went something like this:

I had a metal ellipse guide that was half the diameter of a circle made so that it had a cylindrical vertical rod about an eighth of an inch in diameter ground to a point at the end.

The curve of the arc on the ellipse guide was lower on the end where the vertical bar was than on the opposite end (which would eventually be what is known as the inside diameter of the coin; in numismatic technical circles this is referred to as the ID).

On a 14-inch-square piece of wood with a hole drilled in the center I would build up a one-inch mound of Plastaline oil-based clay. Then I would rake the top of the clay so that it was as flat and even across the top surface as I could make it.

I would then roughly cut an 11-inch-diameter circle around the outside of the clay using a circle compass with a long arm, from the center of the board where the hole was drilled. At this point I had a circular mound of clay approximately one inch thick on the wooden board, with a center hole.

I would then take the ellipse guide, center it over a predetermined center point of the clay, insert the pointed rod through the clay and into the hole in the board, and begin swinging it around, scraping the clay as I swiped. I kept at this until I had formed a concave basin in the clay three-eighths to one-half inch thick, depending on the curvature of the ellipse guide.

Once this was completed I placed a metal band around the concave clay basin, fastened it, and poured plaster over it. After the plaster had dried it was separated, exposing a convex negative model. This model was then sanded and smoothed and refined, creating what was believed to be a smooth negative basin. It was then put on a lathe and trued up to the best of our abilities.

If, in fact, measurements were then taken North, South, East, and West on that basin you probably would have found variations in measurements as great as 30 or 40 thousandths of an inch. In the world of minting, thousandths of an inch are mountains—and at that time, trying to achieve a true basin (one that was even on all four axes, North, South, East, and West) was virtually impossible. We would get close but we could never achieve a true basin. Later on we manufactured ellipse guides that were half the diameter of a circle and mounted them on lathes to true up the convex negative models, but even that did not make a perfect basin, because they had to be touched up by hand—and once you sand a plaster basin by hand it's virtually impossible to true up.

WEINMAN'S WALKING LIBERTY

"The winner of the 1916 design contest for a new half dollar was A.A. Weinman, also the winner of the competition for the dime," numismatic historians Ron Guth and Jeff Garrett write in *United States Coinage: A Study by Type*. "The grace and beauty of Weinman's half dollar design makes it one of the most popular of all American types." These beautiful coins were minted from 1916 through 1947 (except for some years during the Great Depression), at the Philadelphia, Denver, and San Francisco mints.

The coin debuted at a time when Europe was at battle. Great Britain, France, and their allies were fighting the German and Austrian empires and the other Central Powers. The United States had not yet declared war (we would remain neutral until April 1917). Weinman's imagery captures some of the spirit of the era: Miss Liberty is proudly draped in the American flag, walking toward the rising sun and holding a bouquet of laurel and oak—symbolic of civil and military glory. Her outstretched hand represents the bestowal of freedom. At the same time, the American eagle strikes a defiant pose, apparently ready to do battle if necessary. The secretary of the Treasury, William Gibbs MacAdoo, described the coin thus: "The design of the half dollar bears a full-length figure of Liberty, the folds of the Stars and Stripes flying to the breeze as a background, progressing in full stride toward the dawn of a new day. . . . The reverse of the half dollar shows an eagle perched high upon a mountain crag, his wings unfolded, fearless in spirit and conscious of his power. Springing from a rift in the

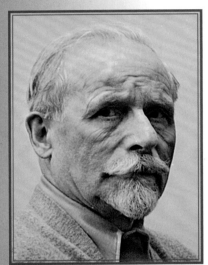

Adolph A. Weinman, designer of the Walking Liberty half dollar, at work in his studio (from *Mehl's Numismatic Monthly*, March 1917) and (above) later in life.

rock is a sapling of mountain pine, symbolical of America."[4]

Guth and Garrett note some technical challenges caused by the design: "Strike is always an issue with this type, especially for those coins struck at the San Francisco Mint. The highest point on the obverse is Liberty's hand; the highest point on the reverse is the eagle's chest and foreleg. Unfortunately, these points oppose each other directly, making it very difficult for metal to flow into the deepest recesses of not one, but two dies. Thus, many of the San Francisco Mint issues, because they were struck with insufficient pressure, looked worn the moment they fell from the dies."[5]

Despite any mechanical troubles in the minting process, Weinman's work stands as a triumph of American numismatics. Art historian Cornelius Vermeule calls it "one of the greatest coins of the United States," noting its "surfaces are formal, like a well-carved marble or precisely cast bronze relief for a war memorial," the detail of the eagle's feathers "is a miraculous coup de force," and as a whole the coin has a "combination of naturalism, classicism, and dignified inner balance, a generally suave figure style in the midst of traditional poses, costumes, and attributes."[6]

Perfect basins would come much later, with the introduction of digital technology. But more about that later.

The basin is critical in the production of a coin. It determines the path where the metal will flow under pressure. If the basin is too deep, the metal won't flow to the edge and fill the cavities of the peripheral design elements (for example, the text). If it's too shallow, or less deep, then the elements on the periphery will fill too soon and the main element in the center of the coin will not fill properly. The harder you strike the coin to get the center element to fill, the more metal will flow to the edge, and you risk getting what's called a fin. A fin is when the metal has no place to go and squeezes out around the die above the top shelf of the coin.

Chief Engraver Gilroy Roberts
working on the Kennedy half dollar.

Gilroy Roberts's obverse design for the John F. Kennedy half dollar.

As far as basins go, I particularly remember the John F. Kennedy half dollar. Gilroy Roberts first made the clay basin, but did not cast it. He began modeling the portrait on the clay basin, and once the portrait was complete he cast them both as one. I wasn't at the Mint at the time but I've seen the model in the Mint's vault.

When the half dollar was minted it became a problem getting the top of Kennedy's head and the hair to form properly, because the basin was too deep where his head met the border. I worked on the top of Kennedy's head (as did every engraver at one time or another), scraping away the detail of the hair and then recutting it at a lower relief in order to get it to fill properly. Then I made a negative model and adjusted the basin.

You can tell after a few setup strikes whether the metal is flowing properly and there is even metal flow all around the coin.

Coin dies typically are processed with two or three alternative basins and tested in pretrial strikes to determine which die, with which basin, gives the best fill so that all elements are clear.

For the first few years of American Silver Eagle production, Weinman's obverse Walking Liberty was used without any modifications, and there were what is referred to in the industry as "fill problems" related to modeling and basin issues. Also, the cry from headquarters was, "We need to see more detail."

There is something in sculpture referred to as "lost and found." This means that you don't have to model all the detail on a piece. All you need to do is create the impression or illusion of an element.

I've never personally been a proponent of going back over a classic model and sharpening the detail. This was how and why John Flanagan's beautiful original obverse quarter portrait (of George Washington) was later referred to as the "Spaghetti Hair." Someone made the determination that they wanted to see every hair on Washington's head.

Nonetheless, detail modifications were made to Weinman's model by defining all the stars in the flag, the oak leaves, the lines in Miss Liberty's skirt, and her sandals, so that everything was as clear as we could make it at that scale.

Production was begun and dies were cut. Unfortunately, the modification hadn't been enough to get the level of detail requested.

Because we were working with six-inch models for both the obverse and reverse, and because we were still using Janvier reducing machines and hadn't yet moved into the digital arena, the artwork was too small for the tracing stylus to get into small areas of the model to pick up fine detail.

Our only option was to enlarge the original model.

The problem with the Janvier machine is that it's made for reducing, and not enlarging. It will create a perfect reduction if the ratios are correct and the artwork is large enough for the stylus to get into the finest element to pick up the

John Flanagan's portrait of George Washington: the original (top), and the modified "Spaghetti Hair" version, redesigned for use on the Mint's State quarters starting in 1999.

detail, but when it comes to enlarging, it's a whole different ball game. Enlargements produced on the Janvier machine look like, for want of a better word, "donuts." All the artwork is overblown and blurred because you can't achieve the proper ratios, thereby requiring recutting and redefining all elements of the model. And that's exactly what we had to do to achieve more detail in the master models.

About 10 years or so into production of the American Silver Eagle we began working with epoxies. Epoxy models were introduced after OSHA deemed it unsafe to use copper or galvano models for Janvier reductions. (Galvanos were the product of electric plating.)

In the older galvano method, first a negative master plaster was made and dried in the oven overnight. The next day, after the model had dried and cooled, it was dusted with copper powder and submerged in a copper electroplating tank filled with active plating fluid. Copper bars hung on one side of the tank and the plaster model (dusted with the copper powder) hung on the opposite side. Copper from the bars found its way to the dusted model and then would adhere to the copper dust and begin to build up.

The model stayed submerged in the electroplating tank for three days, and then it was removed. The plaster was then separated from the copper and you had a positive galvano, which was next cleaned and mounted on the Janvier, where it produced a positive steel reduction.

The problem with galvanos is that you could only use them twice at the most, because copper is soft and the stylus would soften detail. The galvano would be removed from the machine, and sent to the engravers for touchup and cleaning (which entailed using files and sandpaper). It was a laborious process that took an inordinate amount of time.

Epoxies, on the other hand, were very easily cast and cleaned, and they could be used three or four times without losing detail. We now could refine the plasters and that refinement was reflected in the epoxy—no touchup required.

In order to increase the size of the American Silver Eagle, we cast two 12-inch blank epoxy models and mounted them onto the Janviers. Tents were constructed around the machines because it was determined that there would be a great amount of dust generated from the cutting process.

A Janvier reducing machine in action.

A hub being engraved for the 2001 Kentucky state quarter.

This page and following: Note the differences in definition in Miss Liberty's skirt, the flag, and other design details.

The models were first cut in epoxy and cast in negative plaster, then recast to finally produce a positive plaster that then could be redefined with detail restored.

In order for me to reproduce the new master I literally had to counterfeit my own coin. To accomplish this I constructed a grid to fit over the original model, then made another grid proportional to the larger model, laid it over the artwork, and, working in small quadrants, I began to redefine all the lost detail.

It took me about two weeks to finally produce a new larger master model that represented the six-inch original American Silver Eagle reverse. The same was done for the obverse, with another staff engraver restoring detail. Once this was completed, we cut new dies that reflected a visual increase in detail.

This process was used until we transitioned into the digital arena.

I want to take a moment here to clarify something. I've often read numismatic articles, talking about dies going into production, using the phrase "dies were sunk." The proper phrase should be "dies were cut." In the 1970s we did sink dies, but we did it for better fill. Dies are case hardened, which means that

they're softer in the middle than they are on the periphery. At that time, when we ran trial strikes prior to production, in some cases we would find that the center element was filling far too fast and the text on the periphery was very light. If tonnage on the press was increased too much we risked the spreading or doubling of the portrait. To clarify: There is a cavity in the center of the die with the portrait. It takes a certain amount of pressure from the press to fill that cavity. If too much pressure is applied then the metal has nowhere to go and begins to back up. A doubling or spread becomes visible around the portrait and related elements within close proximity. All this is taking place and the text on the edge of the coin is still not formed. This is all related to the height of the basin. That means that the convex dome of the die is too high and had to be lowered so that metal would flow more evenly, enabling the coin to form equally across the surface. To remedy this problem we would "sink the die." The die was tempered or softened and was placed in a press. A piece of lead or soft steel was placed on top of it and pressure applied. If done correctly, you could drop the basin enough to increase even metal flow. You could also explode the die or crack it. It's not a recommended procedure, but under time constraints it was quicker than going back and making a new reduction. It didn't always work but sometimes it did. If it worked a positive metal hub could be manufactured and from that corrected dies with proper basins could be made for production.

A SAMPLING OF AMERICAN EAGLES

Reverse of Augustin Dupré's 1792 Diplomatic medal, commemorating the Declaration of Independence.

Reverse of the half disme of 1792, possibly engraved by Robert Birch.

Reverse of the Draped Bust, Small Eagle silver dollar, by Robert Scot.

Reverse of the Draped Bust, Heraldic Eagle silver dollar, by Robert Scot.

Reverse of the Capped Bust half dollar, early 1800s, by John Reich.

Reverse of Christian Gobrecht's silver dollar of 1836.

Reverse of the Classic Head half eagle ($5 gold coin) of the 1830s, designed by Christian Gobrecht.

A pattern half dollar, by Gobrecht, 1839.

Reverse of the Liberty Seated dollar (1840s–1870s), by Gobrecht.

Reverse of the trade dollar of the 1870s and 1880s, designed by William Barber.

Reverse of the 1878–1921 silver dollar, designed by George T. Morgan.

Reverse of the quarter dollar of 1892–1916, by Charles E. Barber.

Design and Preparation of the Reverse

Throughout numismatic history the eagle has been the one element that probably has been interpreted and reinterpreted more than any other.

Reverse of the half eagle of 1908–1929, by Bela Lyon Pratt.	Reverse of the Standing Liberty quarter dollar of 1916–1930, by Hermon A. MacNeil.	Reverse of Adolph A. Weinman's half dollar of 1916–1947.	Reverse of the 1921–1935 silver dollar, designed by Anthony de Francisci.

Reverse of the double eagle ($20 gold coin) of 1907–1933, by Augustus Saint-Gaudens.	Reverse of the 1918 Illinois Centennial half dollar, by John R. Sinnock.	Reverse of the 1921 Alabama Centennial half dollar, by Laura Gardin Fraser.	Reverse of the Washington quarter dollar (1932–1998), by John Flanagan.

"What might have been": a study for the reverse of the Washington quarter, by John Flanagan.	Obverse of the 1934–1938 Texas Independence Centennial half dollar, by Pompeo Coppini.	Obverse of the 1935 Connecticut Tercentenary half dollar, by Henry G. Kreis.	Reverse of the 1936 Bridgeport, Connecticut, Centennial half dollar, by Kreis.

The Mint Act of 1792 stated that the reverse of the first coin would depict an eagle, the national bird of the United States. Since then the eagle has appeared a multitude of times on U.S. coins and medals. Early eagles have a beautiful folk-art look. They're extremely primitive and reflect the artwork of that period.

The eagle has been installed on shields, over shields, and around shields. Flying, soaring, sitting perched, holding laurel and holly and arrows, looking left, looking right, and (in the case of my 1991 Mount Rushmore Golden Anniversary $5 gold coin) carrying carving tools to the mountain.

I didn't want a flying eagle for the American Silver Eagle coin. I didn't go in the direction of soaring eagles with sun rays behind them because it had been done so many times before. I wanted something more formal; more heraldic.

As I think back on the program, I may have submitted an eagle in flight. The drawings are gone and probably lost forever.

Just a bit of an aside: Many years ago I noticed that drawings that I and the staff were submitting to headquarters were never being returned to the Philadelphia engraving office. One day when I was down in Washington on business I inquired to someone about the problem. They took me aside and quietly whispered in my ear that someday we might be famous and the originals would fetch a good price from collectors, so they were keeping them aside. Needless to say, they never received an original from me after that. This happened at the beginning of my career and since then things have changed dramatically; I know that all our original drawings are now on file where they should be. (Today there are no "original drawings," so to speak; all drawings are produced on computer using Photoshop and Illustrator.)

I submitted two variations of the eagle that ultimately was produced. The first was as it appears on the coin today: formal, facing forward with wings spread wide, 13 stars in a reversed triangle over the eagle's head. This was always my favorite. The second version was the same pose but the eagle was turned slightly to the right, giving it a little perspective.

I don't recall how long we had to work on the American Silver Eagle designs. I would say that, because of the extremely tight deadline, we were allotted no longer than two weeks for finished designs to be submitted.

A sketch for the American Silver Eagle reverse—very close to the design ultimately chosen for the coin.

A related sketch, with the heraldic eagle turned slightly to the viewer's right.

Another sketch, with the legends moved around.

After completing the designs, the established protocol was followed and they were sent to headquarters for review and modification requests. I was notified that my formal design with the eagle facing forward was selected with no modifications and that I should proceed with generating a model for production.

Knowing that the Weinman obverse was six inches required that I make my model the same size. We did this so that we would get the same quality on both sides when we made the Janvier reductions. It was no easy task modeling something so intricate at that scale. It took about two weeks. Dies were then produced and cleaned, and we went into production.

A model of the American
Silver Eagle reverse (cropped).

John Mercanti at work on a
large model of the American
Silver Eagle reverse.

ENGRAVING, DIE PREPARATION, AND CLEANING

After Frank Gasparro left the Mint in 1981 I was, at that time, the last hand engraver on staff. (At the time of this writing there are two steel-die engravers on staff who clean all production-coinage dies. They are also highly skilled at hand engraving.)

The Mint staff in the early 1970s did a large amount of hand engraving directly on medals, where we would engrave the recipient's name. We engraved on bronze, silver, and gold. Not an easy skill to master but once you do it's extremely rewarding.

Unbeknownst to most, metal is like clay. It can be moved. Holes can be filled and errors can be corrected, if not too severe. These corrections are made with various punches. There's much tapping, a lot of metal movement, and a fair amount of sanding.

If a particular program would require the staff to engrave medals, we would first mount them in nests on engraver's vises. The room was always quiet. It took all our concentration to manipulate the vise and swing the graver. Our tools were extremely sharp and in the process of engraving a particular recipient's name on a medal the tools would dull to some degree and would have to be resharpened. Silver wasn't too bad; we might be able to get through the whole name without retouching the tool. But gold was another story. Gold dulls the tool very quickly and it requires an inordinate amount of redressing. We would try to get the most out of a tool before we redressed, and that's where we ran into trouble. You have to redress the tool often when you're cutting gold.

Frank Gasparro, in a relief medallion by Michael Iacocca.

The U.S. Mint's engravers, early in John Mercanti's career: Frank Gasparro, Matthew Peloso, Philip Fowler, Sherl Winter, Mercanti, Edgar Steever, and Michael Iacocca.

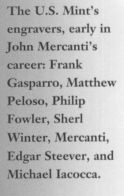

Periods when the staff had projects that required hand engraving were the few times that there was no levity in the department. This was serious business. No papers rattling, no music or eating. Just focusing on the job at hand. The office was as quiet as a tomb. We might be working for a half hour or so, feeling that we were getting through the program with no problems, when we'd hear "@#%&*!" Then tap, tap, tap, tap, as the perpetrator of the error tried desperately to correct his mistake. It might take longer to fix the problem than it took to carve the recipient's name. The quantity of medals was limited, especially if they were gold; only so many would be struck.

Every member of the staff made an error cut at one time or another. It was part of the job.

Then there's die cleaning. It took me about six months to really become proficient at die cleaning. It entailed using a sharp Arkansas stone and various paste abrasives to clean off all the concentric circles left on the artwork from the Janvier reduction process. It took a delicate touch not to obliterate fine detail. I must have gone through a hundred condemned practice dies before I began to pick it up.

Condemned dies are dies of all denominations and programs that are inspected and for some reason or another are not fit to go into production. Any number of things could be wrong with them: they might have gouges or scratches; there could be doubling. They're set aside and ultimately destroyed. I would regularly use them to practice on.

There was a gentleman who was in charge of the die shop, during my formative years, by the name of John Nicolardi—a man of medium build, and very powerful from years of moving heavy metal around. His voice would echo from one end of the die shop to another. You knew when John was upset.

A Mint technician inspecting a die for quality.

He was also a demanding taskmaster. Every production die went through his office to be checked and inspected.

One day John said to me that it was time I start cleaning production dies and stop playing around with condemned dies, which up to that time I had been practicing on. He reached into a box of obverse dime dies, took one out, handed it to me, and said, "Clean it and don't mess it up."

This was the moment I'd been training for up to that point.

I took the die back to my desk and inserted it in the engraver's vise, secured it, and with my hands shaking began to clean it with a stone and abrasives. When I reached a point that I thought it was cleaned I returned to John, who took it to an inspection station and looked at it under a microscope.

He rotated the die around, tilted it for a different light source, looked up at me over the eyepieces, and bellowed, "Not good enough! Take it back and work on it some more."

This went on for I don't know how many times—and for how many dies—until my skills improved and I developed more confidence. What I was really trying to achieve was John's approval. I knew that if he was satisfied with my cleaning skills, I could clean anything that came across my desk. He taught me the proper methods and techniques used in die cleaning. He taught me what abrasives to use and how to use them. Under him I became proficient. He was one of my early mentors who I'll always be indebted to.

All the silver bullion dies that were cut on the Janvier had to be hand cleaned. This is the case even today in the era of digital technology. All dies are hand cleaned but in today's world they don't need to be cleaned as extensively as in the past. Digital technology produces a far better reduction than we had in the era of the Janviers.

The American Silver Eagle obverse and reverse have an enormous amount of detail and required an extensive amount of cleaning.

Another problem with the Janvier machines was repeatability. In a program like the American Silver Eagle it was extremely hard to get multiple reductions that were exactly the same. Every time you set up the artwork it was a little different. Measurements always varied slightly. Sometimes there were considerable variations. Heights of relief might differ. Basin measurements might vary. This all had to do with the fact that every machine was unique. Each machine was an assemblage of levers and pulleys that had to be coordinated just right, and reduction ratios had to be established; consequently, the final product generated on every machine was slightly different to some degree, in every case.

Our transfer engravers (the men in charge of operating the Janvier machines and producing the steel reductions that ultimately would generate the tooling that would create the product) were constantly performing maintenance and tweaking. It was a never-ending job. These men are the unsung heroes of numismatics. They're required to produce tooling that replicates all the detail the designer/sculptor has put into the master model—no easy task then or now, I assure you. It requires one of the highest skill levels in the process, especially today with computer technology and the complex programs that are required to generate cutter paths for the machines that make the final product. There is a great debt owed to every one of them.

Both sides of the American Silver Eagle are intricately detailed, which requires frequent and careful cleaning of the dies.

DIGITAL TECHNOLOGY

As I begin this section I want to make clear that the events I describe may not have occurred exactly in the sequence I relate. To the best of my recollections this is what happened.

On or around the year 2003, under the directorship of Henrietta Holsman Fore, there suddenly appeared in the Mint a young engineer by the name of Steve Antonucci. I would go into the chief engraver's office and see Steve working on his laptop, not really knowing what his official capacity was. He was on board for weeks before I even had a proper introduction. Little did I know how he would ultimately change the face of numismatics in the Mint as far as die production, preparation, and Proof polishing were concerned.

Steve had been hired by headquarters as a private contractor to begin the transition from the standard drawing, modeling, and reduction process to digital technology. This was not going to be easy. There was a great amount of resistance—from older members of the staff and a few individuals who couldn't see the benefits of digital technology—but the decision had been made, and in spite of the pushback we were resolved to move forward.

My immediate supervisor gave me a mandate, in jest: "Those machines will go to the Smithsonian or you will." That pretty much sealed the fate of the Janviers as far as I was concerned.

They had to go.

As an organization, we were increasing our workload every year. Congress was approving more programs than ever. There was our normal circulation-coin workload that consisted of date changes for all denominations, and the ever-increasing commemorative and medal programs. To accomplish all of this we were still using 19th-century technology. We were modeling by hand on old plaster basins and still producing reductions on Janvier machines.

A major problem with the Janvier was that you were never guaranteed a good-quality reduction on the first go-round. There were times the transfer engravers had to make as many as 20 reductions before they had tooling that was good enough to forward to the engravers for cleaning. That certainly would not suffice in this new age.

Something had to be done.

One of our Mint engineers, Barry Claybrook, had been to a show on machine tooling and he saw milling machines that he thought could be used in the coining process. He returned to headquarters and pitched his idea, and this was the genesis that ultimately led us into the digital age.

We had an old Bostomatic milling machine in storage at our Denver mint, and we decided to bring it to Philadelphia for testing. The machine had been sitting in storage out in Denver for a number of years. It wasn't the newest technology and getting parts to refurbish it would be a problem. We had it shipped to Philadelphia and it was eventually brought online. Parts were obtained wherever possible or manufactured in house.

In the early 2000s, the U.S. Mint's workload was growing. The number of regular circulating coins, new State quarters, commemoratives, and medals added to the pressure to move to digital technology.

The Mint director's medal for Henrietta Holsman Fore.

These photographs illustrate the potential variation in mintmark locations—within certain tolerances.

We determined that the Mint director's medal for Henrietta Holsman Fore would be a good project to move forward with digitally. An outside sculptor working in the toy industry was contracted to model the design in virtual reality. It was a slow, tedious process, but he eventually produced a decent digital model that we could move forward with. Our engineers took everything they learned from that process and built on it. The organization had jumped from the 19th century to the 21st and didn't look back.

Once I saw what our engineers had accomplished with the Fore medal I wanted to do something with coinage dies. I asked Steve if, with his milling machine, he could cut in a mintmark on a master die. He looked at me from across my desk where he was sitting and said, "John, I could do this."

We went to the die vault, where I gave him a 50-cent master die. He did the programming and made all the necessary calculations, and the next day I had on my desk a master die with a digitally cut mintmark. I don't recall whether it was an S or a D. It doesn't matter. That small mintmark was the longest leap we had taken so far in digital coinage production. We had replicated something that we were using in production, and it was good enough to move forward with.

Up to that time all mintmarks had been struck by hand. As an example: If we were producing Denver dies, the die shop would bring me a soft master die without a mintmark. I would secure it in the engraver's vise and hand-punch a D into it. The mintmark could only be within a pre-established area of the die. It also had to be vertical with the date. Every engraver had a set of drawings with described tolerances that showed mintmark locations—and God forbid you struck the mintmark out of the specific locations.

The die would then be cleaned, sent to the furnaces for hardening, and re-cleaned, and a production hub would be struck. That in turn would be used to produce Denver production dies.

I was the only engraver on staff who had experience mintmarking dies, and until we moved into digital technology I would still be called on periodically to mintmark a die for production.

Making sure the punch was vertical and in the right location was not an easy task, especially if the task wasn't performed every day. I remember in the late 1970s, when we were still mintmarking dies by hand, it could take all morning to complete the process. Every morning the die shop would roll in to the engraving studio, carts piled high with boxes of dies, 25 dies in a box, all denominations, cents, nickels, dimes, quarters, and half dollars. On some mornings there might be as many as 50 boxes waiting to be mintmarked. These took priority over all other work. The die shop needed these dies mintmarked ASAP so that they could meet their production schedules.

After a number of months mintmark punches would wear or, in most cases, break. New ones had to be made, and they were all made by hand. We took the existing mintmark and made a matrix. A flat piece of soft steel about a half-inch thick with the mintmark P, D, or S punched into it was hardened. A bar of soft steel about a quarter of an inch square was cut to about a four-inch length. It was then ground to a point on one end. The pointed end was flattened slightly. The matrix was secured into an engraver's vise and the four-inch soft ground steel bar was positioned vertically over the secured matrix and the selected mintmark. The bar was then lightly punched, creating a soft image of the mintmark on the tip. The bar was then placed into the vise and the image of the letter was gently nursed out using files, gravers, and abrasives. The bar might be punched into the matrix three or more times and reworked to obtain an image capable of meeting production standards. This process itself could take a week. When the new mintmark was completed, it was sent to heat treating to be hardened.

There were risks in the hardening process. Sometimes the bar would crack in the furnace and the whole process would have to start over. There were times we received a mintmark back from heat treating thinking it was hardened and it wasn't. We'd strike a die and it would collapse. After expending our anger, we'd start the whole process over.

That's why this little task of cutting the mintmark digitally into the die was so important. The engineers knew that if they could locate such a small element on a die and cut it, they could do much more.

This mintmark was an incredible leap forward for us.

My supervisor at this time at our headquarters office in Washington, D.C., sent me a web site related to digital sculpting. The name of the company was Freeform. They had developed a program and a device that enabled the user to sculpt in virtual reality. At the outset the program lent itself more to industrial design, but we saw the potential and purchased a seat (software access for one user) for about seven or eight thousand dollars. As it turned out, it was just what we needed, and ultimately we would buy almost ten seats.

The problem was the learning curve. We would have to isolate a sculptor and we couldn't at that time afford to take a person offline; our schedule was brutal. Steve confided to me that in order for us to make any headway we would either have to train someone on staff or find a digital sculptor. The decision was made to find one, and he did. He found a young sculptor by the name of Joseph Menna, who was working at the Johnson Atelier in Princeton, New Jersey. He joined the Mint's staff in 2005.

As it turned out, Joe was just what the doctor ordered. He was classically trained in sculpture here in America and studied for some years in Russia, where he met his wife. He had been working at the Johnson Atelier using the technology for some time. He became a teacher and a mentor to the Mint's staff in everything related to digital sculpting. I nicknamed him the "Yoda" of the new technology.

Freeform and the related programs we used for modeling are geometric modeling disciplines. Joe knew his way around them better than anyone. We isolated him and allowed him to experiment with various programs. Eventually he was modeling portraits in virtual reality. His knowledge, inquisitiveness, and ability to adapt and utilize multiple programs ultimately enabled us to move forward. He became the cornerstone of the sculpting department.

I remember one night watching the movie "Shrek" with my grandson and after the movie watching the special features. I saw how they constructed the images of the characters in the film and that they were using programs that Joe had been testing. It looked to me as though these programs could be used for modeling coins and medals.

The next day I called the West Coast, made some inquiries, established connections, and, some weeks later, had an artist who worked with these new sculpting programs come to Philadelphia to work with my staff. We were on our way.

Two D (for Denver) mintmarks on Kennedy half dollars—the 1999 made by hand, and the 2009 made digitally.

A sampling of coins designed and sculpted by Joseph Menna.

It also became apparent that we couldn't move forward with the Bostomatic milling machine. Originals were not available anymore and parts had to be manufactured, so we started a worldwide search for new state-of-the-art machines.

Non-sensitive data was established by Steve Antonucci, Barry Claybrook, and their crew of technicians. We sent the data out around the world to various companies who in turn supplied us samples. Our staff of sculptors, engineers, and technicians then evaluated the samples for quality and cleanability. Every sample we received was brought into my office for cleaning. The length of time it took to clean a die just off the milling machine was a major factor, along with the quality of the reduction. With the Janvier machines you had one tool to cut the die. The cutting tool started in the center of the hub and ran in a circular motion out to the edge, producing an image that had concentric circles running throughout. These circles had to be very carefully cleaned off the image using stones and abrasives, producing a final product that was clear, retained all necessary detail, and reflected the intent of the sculptor or designer. Believe me, this is no easy job. As I mentioned earlier, at the beginning of my career I went through hundreds of dies obliterating images and detail.

With digital milling machines a number of tools are used to produce a reduction. All the tool paths are calculated and written by the transfer engravers. Tool paths can be horizontal, vertical, or diagonal. There may be a roughing tool to rough out the artwork . . . a finer tool to cut the portrait . . . and a very fine tool to clean up all imperfections over the finished artwork. Because there are multiple tools, the quality of the final product is far superior to that of the Janvier machines, thereby requiring less cleaning time for the engraver.

We decided on a company by the name of Micron, out of Switzerland. They furnished the best sample that we knew we could improve and build on. Our standards were extremely high. We were fast becoming the world leaders in this technology. Ultimately we purchased six machines, which are now online.

We proved we could manufacture a medal and in the following weeks produced a few prototype dies, multisided and round, but we now had to advance to the next level, which was to produce a coinage die as good as or better than our standard dies, enabling us to move into digital die production.

Which of our coins would serve as our prototype—the first in the new digital age? As it turned out, the coin selected was the American Silver Eagle.

I must pause here for a moment to describe another tool we obtained that is critical to the process: a digital scanner. It was one of the first components we purchased. The scanner enables the user to scan a product—in this case, plaster artwork—into virtual reality, where it can be manipulated. Elements can be added, subtracted, or altered. A scanner is a vital component in this new age because it enables members of the staff who don't feel comfortable modeling on screen in virtual reality, and who still prefer the tactile feeling of modeling in clay, to continue to model the old way. Once the model is completed it's finished in plaster. A final master cast is produced and then scanned into the computer. Once in the computer, cleanup, texturing, or minor modifications can be made.

Let me divert again for a brief second to explain something: I have grossly simplified the whole digital process in this section. It's not my intent to furnish the reader with a thesis on digital technology. I'm not qualified to do that; Steve Antonucci has already provided it. The same with laser Proof polishing: a gentleman by the name of Ron Collins has written that. Ron was brought in as a contractor and was our guru on laser technology. He worked extremely hard bringing laser Proof polishing online. Developing these processes took an extraordinary amount of time and labor, resulting in long days and late nights and great financial expense. The programs for the milling machines, laser machines, and developing the artwork are extremely complicated. These are extremely bright and dedicated and talented individuals, and we wouldn't have made the strides we did without them at the helm. On a far simpler level, I'm describing what we're capable of doing with various elements of this new technology.

We scanned the American Silver Eagle plasters into the computer. All the elements were segregated. Separate files were created for the text and the artwork. A new basin was constructed and images adjusted to fit on the new virtual basin. At the time I modeled the original artwork I didn't use a standard alphabet; a font close to the original was used. Ultimately this caused a problem that resulted in the manufacture of an error coin (or, more accurately in numismatic language, a die variety). The letter U in the selected font had a bar on one side and didn't curve around like my original.

The American Silver Eagle's reverse lettering style of 1986–2007. Note the lack of a spur or stem at the bottom right of the U in UNITED.

Once the new artwork was created in virtual reality, calculations were made for the reductions and they were cut. Eventually dies were struck from the digital reductions and sent to West Point for minting. The year was 2007, and the dies were dated 2008. Both Philadelphia and West Point were instructed to purge their inventory of Janvier-cut dies. Unfortunately, not all the 2007 reverse dies were purged out at West Point. Some still remained in their inventory. They were inadvertently put into the mix at the striking of the 2008 American Silver Eagles and resulted in a number of 2008 coins that had 2007 reverses—a variety that was a boon to the collecting fraternity.

LASER PROOF POLISHING

For years Proof polishing has probably been the most labor-intensive element of coin production. Proof polishers would have to tape and cut around all elements of the production die to protect these concave areas from being polished as they worked on the surface of the dies. A good Proof polisher could only produce a small number of dies in a day.

The reverse lettering style of 2008 to date. Note the spur at the bottom right of the U.

I remember in 1984 attending a chief engravers' conference in Wales. Elizabeth Jones couldn't make it and sent me in her place. One of the stops on the tour of the British Royal Mint was the Proof polishing division. I was astounded to see that they were exclusively using wood tools to accomplish their task—it might take them a day to produce just two Proof polished production dies. True, their production numbers were far below those of the United States, but it was still an extremely long and labor-intensive process. At that time in the United States we used similar methods and techniques; the only difference was that we used electric polishers. Little did we know that there were new processes to come in the world of Proof polishing.

Barry Claybrook found a machine capable of polishing 25 dies at a time to a Proof gloss. It was called a Gerber polisher. A horsehair brush with the aid of abrasives was capable of polishing a box of 25 production dies in minutes. Barry, working together with Ron Collins, eventually developed a process of laser Proof polishing.

American Silver Eagle dies.

In the past, dies selected for Proof polishing were first sandblasted (with sand; later, ceramics were used). The goal of Barry and Ron was to texture the dies with a laser machine, producing a surface that mimicked sandblasting. No easy task, because the laser produced a discernible pattern, and no matter at what angle you viewed it, it still looked like a pattern. With Ron's dedication, hard work, and long hours of experimentation, things began to change and the laser pattern became less detectable. At my retirement at the end of 2010 they were well on their way to producing a scattered pattern that had more of the effect of sand.

The key element in laser Proof polishing is a mask. It is generated from the drawing and model and programmed into the laser. It tells the laser what areas are to be textured on the die and what areas are to be left polished.

A box of 25 dies is first put into the Gerber machine and the dies are polished. They are then taken to the laser, where a technician has a program related to that particular commemorative or denomination. The mask related to that coin is part of that program. The dies are then run through the laser and one by one the dies are textured. They're all exactly alike; repeatability is one of the major benefits of digital technology. The dies may then be touched up by hand if needed.

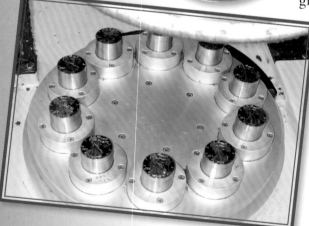

Dies prepared for polishing.

★ ★ ★ ★ ★
★ ★ ★ ★
★ ★ ★
★

I hope what I have described in this chapter gives the reader a better understanding not only of the history of the American Silver Eagle, but also what's involved in their production. Also, I hope you will have a better appreciation not only of the beauty of the piece, but also the time and effort that went into creating it.

I had the honor for 36-plus years of working with the most talented and dedicated people in the history of numismatics. I also had the honor of apprenticing under one of the giants in the field, Frank Gasparro. He taught me how to engrave, how to model, and how to design. In my studio today there is a picture of two men who most influenced me in my life. It's Frank and my father standing side by side. I look at it often and think back on all those years, and wonder where the time went. I'll always be grateful to both: one for giving me life, and the other for giving me a career.

In my tenure, we at the Mint literally went from 19th-century to 21st-century technology. It was an incredible journey. There are no people like Mint people, and to have been a part of that family for all those years is something I will always cherish. I will always remember my first day and my last. They're branded in my soul—as are all the years in between. Someday I hope to tell the story of all those in-between years, the good and the bad. It is my hope, dear reader, that you will want to hear it.

The photograph John Mercanti keeps in his studio, showing his father, Samuel Mercanti (left), and his mentor, Chief Engraver Frank Gasparro.

3
Coin-by-Coin Study of American Silver Eagles

This chapter sets each American Silver Eagle within its historical context and gives collectors an insightful market overview. Each coin is identified by its date, mintmark (if any), and format (i.e., *bullion strike* for the coins produced for bullion sales; or *Proof, Reverse Proof, Burnished,* or *Enhanced Uncirculated* for those formats). Mintages are specified. The mint facilities that produced each coin are noted. Enlarged photographs of each coin are provided, along with relevant close-ups and other related images. The charts include data on how many coins have been certified by PCGS in Mint State and Proof conditions up to 70; and values in several conditions.

A note about spotting: White spots have been known to occasionally appear on American Silver Eagles (as they do on other .999 silver coins)—sometimes shortly after minting, sometimes weeks or months later. Not every coin will develop such spots, but they do show up with some frequency, and buyers should be aware of the possibility. For more information, see the related appendix.

A note about First Strike, Early Release, and similar designations: The U.S. Mint does not have a program or designation for the first or earliest coins struck by a set of dies, or for the coins produced first or earliest in a particular year or series. PCGS and NGC designate American Silver Eagles packaged and delivered by the Mint within 30 days of initial sales as *First Strike* or *Early Release*. The coins must be shipped by their owner to the grading firm postmarked within the cutoff date, and in their original sealed packaging. Extra fees apply for certification with these designations. More details can be found online at www.PCGS.com and www.NGCcoin.com.

1986, BULLION STRIKE
Mintage: 5,393,005

Minted at San Francisco, Denver, and West Point, without mintmark

Historical context: In the financial arena of the mid-1980s, unwise lending strategies of some banks, and poor oversight of savings and loans institutions, led to turmoil and the closing of many banks.

The debut year of the American Silver Eagle, 1986, was also the year the Professional Coin Grading Service (PCGS) began operation as a third-party grading service. That summer, the American Numismatic Association added numbers to its official grading standards (which previously consisted of text descriptions only), including 11 Mint State increments from low-end MS-60 to perfect MS-70. Hobby periodical *Coin World* boasted a circulation of 80,394 subscribers; *COINage* magazine, 60,367; *Numismatic News*, 35,923; and *The Numismatist* (official magazine of the ANA), 33,072. Gold as bullion was priced in the New York market at an average of $368.24 per ounce for the year.

1986 average silver price: $5.47/ounce.

Coin commentary: In its first year of issue, a new coin will often be popular with collectors as well as curious members of the general public. The first American Silver Eagle was no exception. The coins were on sale only in the final weeks of 1986, in late November and December, and it took a mintage of more than 5 million to satisfy demand. The West Point, Denver, and San Francisco mints were put to work to turn out so many coins; no mintmarks were used to distinguish their sources, although some coins have been authenticated as being from the "First Strike" ceremony at the San Francisco Assay Office presided over by Secretary of the Treasury James Baker (see chapter 1).

The popular 1986 bullion strike has remained affordable since its debut.

The coin was ranked no. 83 in the third edition of *100 Greatest U.S. Modern Coins* by Schechter and Garrett, who call it "the coin that started it all."

1986	<MS-65	MS-65	MS-66	MS-67	MS-68	MS-69	MS-70	Total
Certified	31	49	119	306	1,119	11,126	36	12,869
Value					$42	$55	$675	

1986-S, PROOF

Mintage: 1,446,778

Minted at San Francisco, with S mintmark

Coin commentary: The 1986 American Silver Eagle has the highest mintage among Proofs in the series, reflecting collector and investor demand for this first-year-of-issue coin. The 1986 Proof was sold by the Mint for $21. Aftermarket premiums have remained modest over the years. Although more than 1,000 examples have been certified at PF-68 and lower, the discerning collector will seek a higher-grade example.

1986-S	<PF-65	PF-65	PF-66	PF-67	PF-68	PF-69	PF-70	Total
Certified	23	35	57	243	1,123	18,944	3,073	23,498
Value					$60	$80	$525	

1987, BULLION STRIKE
Mintage: 11,442,335

Minted at Philadelphia, without mintmark

Historical context: 1987 was the first year American Silver Eagles were available for sale from January through December. (The debut issue of 1986 was on sale only in the closing weeks of that year.) The U.S. Mint had awarded a contract to Grey Advertising of New York City to assist in publicizing and marketing the bullion coins, globally as well as in the home market. These efforts were expanded in 1987. Numismatic Guaranty Corporation of America (NGC) was launched as a third-party grading firm this year.

Silver's bullion value peaked above $10 per ounce during 1987, and averaged out to about $7 by year's end. Like silver, gold also averaged higher than it did in 1986—about $80 per ounce higher, at $447.95.

1987 average silver price: $7.02/ounce.

Coin commentary: Demand for the 1987 bullion strike was high, and the coin's mintage surpassed 11.4 million—a record that would stand for more than 20 years.

A so-called "monster box" (15 x 8.5 x 4.5 inches) of American Silver Eagles.

1987	<MS-65	MS-65	MS-66	MS-67	MS-68	MS-69	MS-70	Total
Certified	57	71	147	388	933	12,212	27	13,840
Value					$30	$45	$1,650	

1987-S, PROOF
Mintage: 904,732
Minted at San Francisco, with S mintmark

Coin commentary: While orders for bullion-strike 1987 American Silver Eagles more than doubled in the series' sophomore year, demand for Proof examples fell by one third. Still, the 1987-S American Silver Eagle Proof has the second-highest mintage of all Proofs minted in the 1980s. The Mint sold the 1987 Proof for $23 (an increase of $2 over the preceding year). Premiums for the 1987-S Proof are typical for a type coin in the series, though the date has traditionally traded at $1,000 or more in PF-70. Since publication of the first edition of this guide, the population of PF-70 coins has more than doubled—in the second edition it was just over 500 coins—so while the 1988 Proof is scarcer, demand for these coins is such that the market continues to hold at historical levels.

Collectors should seek spot-free specimens with thick and consistent cameo frosting and rich black mirrors, while avoiding coins that exhibit imperfections, such as haze or milk spots. Pieces with vivid toning can also be found.

1987-S	<PF-65	PF-65	PF-66	PF-67	PF-68	PF-69	PF-70	Total
Certified	16	27	48	172	746	11,796	1,407	14,212
Value					$60	$85	$1,000	

1988, BULLION STRIKE

Mintage: 5,004,646

Minted at Philadelphia, without mintmark

Historical context: The stock market crash of October 1987 did little to shake the fundamentals of the American economy, which continued to grow. Some investors looking to outperform the stock market turned their attention to rare coins. Some investment firms went so far as to establish rare-coin funds.

Grading, then as now, was an important part of coin collecting. In Chicago in May 1988 the American Numismatic Association scheduled a three-day seminar on how to grade rare coins.

The emergence of third-party grading services and the promise of standardized grading helped fuel this growth segment within the hobby. Unfortunately, buying and selling rare coins for profit requires highly technical knowledge and a nuanced understanding of numismatics.

Wealthy novice collectors sometimes found themselves the victims of unscrupulous dealers and telemarketers. To combat this, the American Numismatic Association and the Federal Trade Commission announced their intention to co-publish a brochure, "Consumer Alert: Investing in Rare Coins," designed to educate consumers interested in the investment side of the hobby.

By the beginning of 1988, nearly 17 million ounces of silver had been absorbed into the marketplace through the American Silver Eagle bullion program. The bullion value of gold was slightly down compared to 1987, averaging $438.31 per ounce for the year, while silver was off more than 7% from its position in 1987.

1988 average silver price: $6.52/ounce.

Coin commentary: Demand for the 1988 issue was less than half that of the previous year, with just over 5 million coins being sold.

The 1988 bullion strike today enjoys a strong premium in the highest Mint State grade, MS-70.

1988	<MS-65	MS-65	MS-66	MS-67	MS-68	MS-69	MS-70	Total
Certified	15	27	74	220	696	6,929	1	7,964
Value					$30	$50	$2,000	

1988-S, Proof

Mintage: 557,370

Minted at San Francisco, with S mintmark

Coin commentary: Demand declined for the 1988-S Proof, with some 347,362 fewer coins being purchased than in 1987. The Mint kept its price steady at $23 per coin.

Although several hundred have been certified at PF-68 and lower, savvy collectors will pursue a higher-level example for their collections.

The year 1988 was significant for the West Point Mint, which had been built in 1937 as the West Point Bullion Depository—a storage facility for silver bullion, nicknamed "The Fort Knox of Silver." According to the Mint's historical literature, "From 1973 to 1986, West Point produced cents, and in 1980 began striking gold medallions. Shortly afterward, approximately 20 billion dollars worth of gold was stored in its vaults, making it second only to Fort Knox for gold storage. Today, it is also the major producer of gold coins."

Continuing: "The red letter date for West Point was March 31, 1988, when it gained official status as a United States Mint."

It would be several more years before the West Point Mint would strike American Silver Eagle coins, as it did in the first year of the series. After the facility's change in status in 1988, its first Proof coin in the silver bullion series would be the famous 1995-W (see page 67).

Today West Point continues as a storage facility, but as a branch mint it also manufactures, packages, and ships gold and silver commemorative coins, as well as American Eagle bullion coins in regular, Proof, and Burnished formats.

The 1988-S Proof American Silver Eagle is actually underrated at PF-70. As of the publication of this book, fewer examples of this coin have been certified PF-70 than any other issue from the 1980s.

1988-S	<PF-65	PF-65	PF-66	PF-67	PF-68	PF-69	PF-70	Total
Certified	7	14	34	77	515	9,318	1,244	11,210
Value					$60	$90	$500	

1989, BULLION STRIKE
Mintage: 5,203,327

Minted at Philadelphia, without mintmark

Historical context: The big international news of 1989 was the fall of the Berlin Wall. News in the United States was dominated by the crash of the oil tanker *Exxon Valdez* and the spilling of its crude oil in Alaska's waters.

Investor money continued to flow into the hobby marketplace in 1989, with interest from Wall Street and fortune-seekers driving the prices of many popular coin series up beyond normal collector levels.

Collectors didn't know it yet, but 1989 represented a peak in the market for silver dollars and other high-visibility coins (the kinds that attracted Wall Street attention). The excitement would cool off over the next several years, but for now the markets were flush with cash.

Coin collecting as a popular hobby made national headlines when some 1989 Washington quarters were discovered without mintmarks (normally a quarter struck for circulation would have either a P mintmark for the Philadelphia Mint, or a D for the Denver Mint). The *New York Times* reported on the phenomenon in its May 27 issue, in a long article headlined "Quarters, Mints and Marks: Little Things Can Mean a Lot." The *Times* noted that "The first quarter minus the mint mark was discovered in Boston by a coin collector and sent to *Numismatic News*, a weekly publication for coin collectors based in Iola, Wis. The publication's editors lent the quarter, on which the second 9 in the 1989 date was partly erased, to the United States Mint for analysis. Eugene H. Essner, the deputy director of the Mint, confirmed that the quarter was genuine.

The *Chicago Tribune* reported on the 1989 coin market in a January 21, 1990, article. "Investors in extremely rare coins enjoyed a profitable 1989, according to comprehensive price surveys compiled by the hobby's two largest newspapers," the *Tribune* noted. "*Coin World*'s Trends Index suggests that rarities in the 'choice uncirculated' category (MS-65) jumped 50.6 percent in value in the 12 months ending Nov. 30. The MS-65 index went up 26.2 percent in 1988 and 13.2 percent in 1987. Likewise, the *Numismatic News* coin index—which tracks prices in 17 areas of the market—went up 45.5 percent in 1989. Experts attribute the strong market . . . to the creation of limited partnerships that invest in rare coins in the top condition categories, and to other factors."

Silver's bullion value was down about $1 per ounce for the year, and gold dropped more than $50, averaging at $382.58.

1989 average silver price: $5.52/ounce.

Coin commentary: Demand for the 1989 bullion issue was slightly stronger than for the 1988, with just over 5.2 million coins sold.

1989 (among other dates) "World Trade Center" American Silver Eagles have been graded and authenticated by PCGS. The coins were certified as being found in a vault pulled from the wreckage at Ground Zero, post-9/11.

1989	<MS-65	MS-65	MS-66	MS-67	MS-68	MS-69	MS-70	Total
Certified	26	42	68	232	1,641	7,110	1	9,121
Value					$30	$50	$1,400	

1989-S, PROOF

Mintage: 617,694

Minted at San Francisco, with S mintmark

Coin commentary: 1989 saw a slight uptick in the number of Proof American Silver Eagles purchased, reversing a two-year decline. Mintage stood at 617,694 pieces. The Mint sold the coins directly to the public for $23 each.

As one might expect, coin quality continued to be excellent out of the gate. However, age and improper storage have marred many specimens over the years. PF-69 is the "typical" grade for certified examples, with only the top 5% or so of certified coins grading PF-70. The term *typical* is misleading, however, since most American Silver Eagles submitted for grading are hand selected for quality.

Expect hazy or discolored coins to grade lower, and avoid buying them as numismatic items.

Attractive toned examples exist, but collectors who prefer the original black-and-white cameo contrast should exercise some discernment. Cameo frosting varies from well frosted to extra thick.

1989-S	<PF-65	PF-65	PF-66	PF-67	PF-68	PF-69	PF-70	Total
Certified	14	20	35	87	400	10,540	2,017	13,112
Value					$60	$90	$325	

1990, Bullion Strike
Mintage: 5,840,210
Minted at Philadelphia, without mintmark

Historical context: Iraq's occupation of oil-rich Kuwait, and the subsequent Gulf War led by the United States, was one of the biggest news stories of 1990. The war's far-reaching impact on geopolitics and energy policy would play out over the course of the next couple decades. Another historic international event, the reunification of East and West Germany, signaled the beginning of the end of the Cold War.

1990 was a pivotal year for the numismatic market as well. The industry was forced to reinvent itself after the Wall Street investment bubble deflated. Easy-to-promote coins, such as high-end commemoratives and silver dollars, suffered the most during this bear market. Collectors' series suffered only minimally, as esoteric and scarce numismatic items retained their core group of buyers.

The American Numismatic Association and the Federal Trade Commission jointly continued to educate consumers about safety in the marketplace. The *Chicago Tribune* in its April 15, 1990, edition reported that nearly 100,000 copies of the ANA/FTC brochure on investing in rare coins had been distributed since 1988. The newspaper further noted that "Numismatic keepsakes outperformed most other types of investments—including stocks and Treasury bills—in the 12 months ending last June 1, according to a widely quoted survey by Salomon Brothers, Inc."

Bullion coins like the American Silver Eagle continued to operate in the market primarily as investment instruments. The spot price of silver was down about 70 cents per ounce on average for the year, while gold remained steady—a couple dollars up from 1989, averaging $384.93 per ounce.

1990 average silver price: $4.82/ounce.

Coin commentary: Demand for the 1990 bullion strike American Silver Eagle increased 12% over the prior year, marking the third consecutive year of increased demand. A majority of the certified population of 1990 American Silver Eagles grades MS-69. Coins designated "First Strike" are elusive for this date.

Like many dates in the series, the 1990 bullion strike features many exquisitely toned coins. These one-of-a-kind treasures can command significant premiums and are desirable for collectors in Mint State regardless of numerical grade.

1990	<MS-65	MS-65	MS-66	MS-67	MS-68	MS-69	MS-70	Total
Certified	58	52	136	315	878	4,628	1	6,069
Value					$30	$50	$1,500	

1990-S, PROOF
Mintage: 695,510

Minted at San Francisco, with S mintmark

Coin commentary: The fifth year of American Silver Eagle Proof production saw a noticeable spike over the past year, with 695,510 coins struck. This benchmark would go unmatched for more than ten years. The U.S. Mint continued to offer the coin to collectors for $23 each.

In PF-70 the 1990-S is the most common of the original run of 1986–1992 San Francisco Mint American Silver Eagles. Since the first edition of this book went to press, population totals for this coin in the ultimate grade have quadrupled. Demand for this coin at the high end remains strong, with pieces trading for more than $200 each. PF-69 coins are readily available and affordable at $90 each. Attractively toned pieces in PF-68 or PF-69 can sell for as much as a perfect black-and-white example!

1990-S	<PF-65	PF-65	PF-66	PF-67	PF-68	PF-69	PF-70	Total
Certified	10	15	36	91	371	10,296	2,675	13,495
Value					$60	$90	$200	

1991, BULLION STRIKE
Mintage: 7,191,066

Minted at Philadelphia, without mintmark

Historical context: Many of the former Soviet states comprising the USSR became independent in 1991. The American economy was strong. In the numismatic market, formerly inflated investment-level prices continued to drop to more realistic levels.

The *Chicago Tribune* in its August 15, 1991, edition ("A Penny Saved May Be Big Deal to Collectors") reported on the American Numismatic Association's summer show, held in Chicago because that's the city the ANA had been founded in 100 years earlier. "In everything from impressive leather bags to emptied cottage cheese containers, all kinds of coins and money-related material came through the center," the *Tribune* observed. "There was the 22-karat gold, 'sailor head, half-eagle' coin, part of the Ed Trompeter collection valued at $10 million. There were wooden coins, miniature coins, quarters the size of dimes, dimes the color of pennies, coins that circulated during biblical days, medals won during the civil war, U.S. Treasury documents signed by Abraham Lincoln and Richard Nixon. There was not, however, any sign of the 1909 and 1914 pennies that had earlier been secretly circulated near the expo center to present a challenge: Anyone who recognizes them and brings them to the convention during its five- day run will receive the $370 and $400 the coins are worth, respectively. But as longtime coin collector Chet Krause said, 'By now, those pennies might be anywhere, in a toll booth or a bubble gum machine.' But maybe not."

Silver bullion was down nearly $1 per ounce for the year. Gold, too, dipped, averaging about $21 less per ounce than 1990, at $363.29.

1991 average silver price: $4.06/ounce.

Coin commentary: The mintage of 1991 bullion strikes hit a post-1986 peak of nearly 7.2 million coins—a record that would hold until near the end of the decade. At the MS-70 level the 1991 has one of the strongest values in the marketplace.

1991	<MS-65	MS-65	MS-66	MS-67	MS-68	MS-69	MS-70	Total
Certified	48	35	98	229	1,475	7,986	0	9,873
Value					$30	$45	$4,400	

1991-S, Proof

Mintage: 511,925

Minted at San Francisco, with S mintmark

Coin commentary: The Mint's issue price of $23 remained in place for 1991 Proofs, but demand fell sharply, to about three-quarters the 1990 level. Even with the decreased sales, the 1991 mintage of 511,925 coins would be a high point until 1999.

With the majority of professionally certified 1991-S American Silver Eagles grading PF-69 and PF-70, a collector with an eye for quality will seek one of those higher levels. The U.S. Mint offers such high-quality collectible products that collectors risk becoming spoiled; any 1991-S Proof American Silver Eagle grading below PF-68 would be considered on the low end of the acceptable scale.

1991-S	<PF-65	PF-65	PF-66	PF-67	PF-68	PF-69	PF-70	Total
Certified	9	9	21	89	454	8,717	1,077	10,376
Value					$60	$80	$450	

1992, BULLION STRIKE
Mintage: 5,540,068

Minted at Philadelphia, without mintmark

Historical context: By 1992 the Wall Street hullaballoo in the coin market had quieted down, allowing collectors—as opposed to investors—to dominate the hobby once again. The American Numismatic Association held its annual springtime National Money Show in Dallas, Texas, and its summer World's Fair of Money in Orlando, Florida.

The price of silver continued to decline, as it had for several years. However, by mid-1992 analysts began to anticipate a rise in silver prices, up to $4.25 per ounce. In the end, silver averaged just under the $4.00 mark for the year. Gold, too, proved to be a loser in 1992, shedding $20 an ounce to average $344.97 for the year.

1992 average silver price: $3.95/ounce.

Coin commentary: The lack of action in the silver market led to a 26% decline in the number of bullion American Silver Eagles struck in 1992. Currently, this issue commands a modest numismatic premium in MS-69.

PCGS and NGC certification data show distributions that significantly favor MS-69. This reflects a high percentage of coins hand-picked for quality before being submitted for grading. Very few MS-70 examples have been certified by the major grading firms—all the more reason for savvy collectors to keep an eye out for those elusive perfect coins.

1992	<MS-65	MS-65	MS-66	MS-67	MS-68	MS-69	MS-70	Total
Certified	25	29	85	187	1,567	6,928	1	8,823
Value					$30	$50	$1,550	

1992-S, PROOF

Mintage: 498,654

Minted at San Francisco, with S mintmark

Coin commentary: 1992 marks the end of the American Silver Eagle's initial seven-year Proof run at the San Francisco Mint. Starting in 1993, American Silver Eagle Proof coinage would be produced at the Philadelphia Mint. American Silver Eagle production didn't return to the "Granite Lady" until 2011.

1992 was also the first year since 1964 that the U.S. Mint struck 90% silver coinage in Proof sets. The 1992-S Silver Proof Set included three coins traditionally struck in 90% silver (the Kennedy half dollar, Washington quarter, and Roosevelt dime), along with the base-metal denominations of the nickel and cent. The set was offered for sale at $37.50. More than a million United States Silver Proof Sets were sold.

1992-S	<PF-65	PF-65	PF-66	PF-67	PF-68	PF-69	PF-70	Total
Certified	5	7	24	49	370	9,184	1,214	10,853
Value					$60	$75	$350	

1993, BULLION STRIKE

Mintage: 6,763,762

Minted at Philadelphia, without mintmark

Historical context: 1993 saw the rare-coin market begin the long road to recovery after the investment bubble burst. High-end coins began to rebound, but still traded well below peak levels.

The American Numismatic Association polled its 28,000 members about current U.S. money, in a mail-in survey published in the June 1993 issue of its monthly magazine, *The Numismatist*. The general consensus was that the cent and the half dollar should be retained (so said nearly two thirds of respondents); that a dollar coin should replace the $1 bill; that at least one side of each circulating coin should be modernized with a new design; and that more color should be used on the nation's paper currency (the latter three opinions voiced by more than half of respondents). The ANA board of governors endorsed a bill in Congress for a golden-colored dollar coin to replace the $1 note.

Two fantastic rarities set auction records this year: the Mickley-Hawn-Queller 1804 dollar sold for more than $475,000 at a Heritage auction and the Olsen-Hawn 1913 Liberty Head nickel (which PCGS has certified at PF-64) sold for $962,500. . . a bargain by today's standards.

Meanwhile, gold and silver prices saw some long-overdue upward movement in 1993. Gold finished the year averaging $360.91 per ounce ($15 higher than 1992 levels), while silver crossed the $4 barrier for good. Bullion-strike American Silver Eagle production rose nearly 20% in 1993, thanks to climbing metals prices.

1993 average silver price: $4.31/ounce.

Coin commentary: MS-70 perfection continues to be elusive, with no examples yet certified at that level. The crop of American Silver Eagles of 1993, like many others of that decade, offers fans of toned coins many pleasing examples. As most of these coins have been removed from original packaging and exposed to the elements, the typical grade dips between MS-66 and MS-68. Plenty of hand-selected MS-68 and MS-69 examples exist, trading for a slight premium over melt.

1993	<MS-65	MS-65	MS-66	MS-67	MS-68	MS-69	MS-70	Total
Certified	54	87	187	452	1,116	4,576	0	6,476
Value					$30	$50	$3,250	

1993-P, PROOF

Mintage: 405,913

Minted at Philadelphia, with P mintmark

Coin commentary: Proof production was moved from San Francisco to the Philadelphia Mint in 1993.

Among regular-issue Proof American Silver Eagles, the 1993-P has the second-lowest mintage, at just over 400,000 pieces. Not surprisingly, it commands a premium over Proofs of the preceding years, especially at the PF-70 level.

The U.S. Mint's issue price for the 1993-P Proof was $23.

Some 1993-P Proof American Silver Eagles were issued in a special package of coins—the Philadelphia Mint Bicentennial Set (see next entry for more details). The Knight Ridder / Tribune syndicate publicized the set in an article entitled "Philadelphia Mint's 200 Years Are Honored": "The U.S. Mint is offering a set of coins to mark the 200th anniversary of the first coins struck at the Philadelphia Mint. The Philadelphia Set, created for collectors, contains three fractional gold Eagle proofs, the silver Eagle proof and a silver medal marking the mint's anniversary. All the proofs and medal bear the 'P' mint mark. The set will be sold only in 1993. It is the first year the Philadelphia Mint has struck the silver eagles, and the last year the Philadelphia Mint will strike fractional gold Eagles. The Philadelphia Set sells for $499." The coins in these sets accounted for nearly 13,000 of the year's Proof American Silver Eagle mintage (out of a total of 405,913).

Eagles from the 1993 Philadelphia Set tend to tone in a unique, pastel-purple toning pattern that starts around the rim and proceeds toward the center of the coin. This is probably the result of exposure to chemicals from the set's packaging. Finding an example of this coin in the original white-and-black is very tough.

1993-P	<PF-65	PF-65	PF-66	PF-67	PF-68	PF-69	PF-70	Total
Certified	27	19	38	162	685	9,398	836	11,166
Value					$85	$120	$1,600	

1993 Philadelphia Mint Bicentennial Set

Mintage: 12,869

Minted at Philadelphia, with P mintmarks

Set commentary: This set was issued to celebrate the 200th anniversary of the first official regular coins struck for general circulation by the U.S. Mint in Philadelphia. It includes three denominations of 1993 American Gold Eagles ($5, $10, and $25, from one-tenth ounce to one-half ounce), plus the 1993 American Silver Eagle. In addition the set includes a .76-ounce, .900 fine silver commemorative medal depicting the famous John Ward Dunsmore painting of Martha Washington inspecting the first U.S. coinage (see *The Secret History of the First U.S. Mint*, by Orosz and Augsburger) and various U.S. coin designs.

The coins and the medal are all in Proof format.

In *American Gold and Silver: U.S. Mint Collector and Investor Coins and Medals, Bicentennial to Date*, Dennis Tucker writes:

Many of the silver medals (and the accompanying American Silver Eagle) have toned over the years from exposure to the heavy green cardboard of the set's packaging. The resulting coloration can be dramatic and visually appealing—of course with beauty being in the eye of the coin holder.

This set was packaged with a green velvet box and a certificate of authenticity. Its issue price was $499.

1993 Set	Proof
Value	$1,725

1994, BULLION STRIKE
Mintage: 4,227,319
Minted at Philadelphia, without mintmark

Historical context: Political instability in Mexico and increased demand from India drove silver upward for the first quarter of 1994. Silver peaked in March at $5.75 per ounce. These gains quickly subsided, and silver was trading below $5.00 by November. While orders for bullion-strike American Silver Eagles were strong in the first half of the year, the decline in precious-metal prices led to weaker demand for the coins in the second half. As a result, sales of 1994 bullion strikes fell by nearly one third in 1994. The issue's total mintage of 4,227,319 is the second lowest among American Silver Eagle bullion strikes.

The coin market, like the U.S. economy as a whole, continued to grow in strength in 1994. Classic American coin prices continued to recover, and the Mint released seven different commemorative designs. This made 1994 the busiest year for the U.S. commemorative program since 1936, when the Mint released an astonishing 21 different coins.

Gold climbed to an average price of $385.42 per ounce for the year, while silver ended 1994 with a yearly average of $5.29 per ounce.

1994 average silver price: $5.29/ounce.

Coin commentary: MS-70 remains the most elusive of grades for the 1994 bullion strike. More than half the coins submitted for professional grading (cherrypicked for quality by their submitters, of course) come close to perfection, grading MS-69. Series specialists observe that the 1994 bullion strike is one of the tougher dates to find in very nice quality. Usually some slight tick or surface mark keeps the issue from reaching higher grades, making the coin slightly underrated at MS-69.

1994	<MS-65	MS-65	MS-66	MS-67	MS-68	MS-69	MS-70	Total
Certified	88	99	274	423	3,701	5,133	0	9,719
Value					$40	$57	$4,500	

1994-P, PROOF
Mintage: 372,168
Minted at Philadelphia, with P mintmark

Coin commentary: The 1994-P has the lowest mintage of any regular-issue American Silver Eagle Proof. (Only the 1995-W, sold by the Mint in special sets rather than individually, has a lower mintage.)

Collectors and investors had cooled on the desirability of Proof American Silver Eagles by 1994; with silver hovering around $5 an ounce as bullion, Proofs could be found on the secondary market for prices lower than the Mint's official issue price of $23 per coin. The Mint sold fewer and fewer of the Proofs each year from 1991 through 1994, until finally they bottomed out at less than 400,000 coins.

The 1994-P Proof was ranked no. 60 in the *100 Greatest U.S. Modern Coins*, third edition, where it is noted that "the 1994 issue has emerged as a key date, often more difficult to locate than the 2006-W Reverse Proof issue, and therefore it can also be more expensive." The coin commands a premium at all collectible levels, with the examples graded at PF-70 being especially valuable.

1994-P	<PF-65	PF-65	PF-66	PF-67	PF-68	PF-69	PF-70	Total
Certified	12	21	55	158	680	8,375	744	10,045
Value					$90	$140	$1,700	

1995, BULLION STRIKE
Mintage: 4,672,051
Minted at Philadelphia, without mintmark

Historical context: In 1995 the federal government's budget was too small to meet expenses, and as the year ended there was the threat of some government services being shut down. Precious metals had their normal ups and downs but held steady. The price of silver surpassed $6 an ounce in May and then had a downward trend. Compared to 1994 the metal averaged a few cents weaker for the year. Gold, meanwhile, averaged out a few cents higher, at $385.50 compared to the previous year's $385.42.

Numismatics made national headlines early in the year when it was publicized that the Willis H. duPont family was donating two famous silver dollars to museums. The coins, dated 1804 but actually made years later from old unused dies, had been stolen from the duPonts in an armed robbery in 1967. One was a Class I specimen, one of only eight struck in the 1830s as official gifts of the United States to be presented to foreign rulers and dignitaries, including the king of Siam. This one was donated to the American Numismatic Association's Money Museum in Colorado Springs, Colorado. The other was a Class III restrike, one of 15 known to have been secretly made at the Mint in the 1850s, using the old dies, for back-door sale to wealthy and well-connected private collectors. This coin was donated to the Smithsonian Institution's National Numismatic Collection. (The story of these coins is told in *The Fantastic 1804 Dollar*, by Eric P. Newman and Kenneth E. Bressett.)

1995 average silver price: $5.19/ounce.

Coin commentary: Demand for the 1995 bullion strike was higher than for the 1994, resulting in 4,672,051 coins being sold.

The 1995 bullion strike offers a dramatic illustration of the fluidity of certification data. When the second edition of this book was published, a single example of the 1995 bullion strike had been graded MS-70 by PCGS. As of press date for the third edition, more than 20 have been graded MS-70. This reality—the fact that today's uniquely perfect coin might have dozens of companions a week, a month, or a year later—acts as a governor on the market prices for MS-70 coins.

1995	<MS-65	MS-65	MS-66	MS-67	MS-68	MS-69	MS-70	Total
Certified	43	46	137	330	2,275	8,368	23	11,222
Value					$38	$57	$750	

1995-P, PROOF
Mintage: 438,511

Minted at Philadelphia, with P mintmark

Coin commentary: The American Silver Eagle entered its 10th year of production in 1995. The U.S. Mint offered two collectible versions of the coin to the public: the standard Philadelphia-minted Proof (issue price $23), and the considerably rarer 1995-W Proof (see next listing).

Mintage of the 1995-P Proof was capped at 500,000. The year's sales came under that limit, to just under 440,000 coins; this quantity was lower than most previous Proofs of the series. Today the 1995-P enjoys a modest secondary-market premium over most other American Silver Eagle Proofs. More than 1,200 have been graded by PCGS at the highest level, PF-70.

A possible reason for the lower mintage than those seen in previous years was that many collectors did not welcome the 1995-W Proof American Silver Eagle, which was only available as part of a set costing $999. In a "Guest Commentary" column published in the June 26, 1995, issue of *Coin World*, Mint Director Philip N. Diehl wrote, "I acknowledge that the $999 purchase price for the 10th Anniversary set with the 1995-W Proof silver Eagle seems high and that not every collector of Proof silver Eagles can afford it. However, that price is more affordable than you might think. I've just finished scanning the 'buy prices' for 1994 American Eagle Proof gold coins in the coin market section of several numismatic publications. I see that collectors can, on average, sell unpackaged, individual Proof gold American Eagles in each of the four denominations to a dealer for $949. And that's an average resale price; by shopping around, you could do better than this." He added, "Using the $949 price as a guide, a single Proof silver Eagle from the 1995 10th Anniversary set has an effective price of $50 for collectors of silver Eagles who buy the five-coin set and immediately sell the four gold coins back to a dealer. Other things being equal, a $50 effective price seems like a reasonable, reachable, and even tempting price for one of the lowest mintage U.S. coins in this century."

In this remarkable statement, Diehl foreshadowed the speculation that would accompany later limited-release U.S. Mint products where some buyers would purchase coins not to add to their collections, but with the hope of flipping them for a quick profit.

1995-P	<PF-65	PF-65	PF-66	PF-67	PF-68	PF-69	PF-70	Total
Certified	11	10	22	94	527	8,300	1,222	10,186
Value					$80	$110	$450	

1995-W, PROOF
Mintage: 30,125
Minted at West Point, with W mintmark

Coin commentary: The 10th year of the United States' bullion coinage program was marked in 1995 by a special set of Proof coins issued by the U.S. Mint. The set included all four denominations of the 1995 American Gold Eagle—the tenth-ounce $5 coin, the quarter-ounce $10, the half-ounce $25, and the one-ounce $50. All were struck at West Point, with a W mintmark. The fifth coin in the set would become known as the "king of the Silver Eagles." Like its gold companions, the silver Proof was minted at West Point and bears that facility's W mark.

There was only one way for collectors to get the 1995-W Proof American Silver Eagle: by purchasing the complete 10th-anniversary set of coins. (The gold Proofs were available individually, but the silver West Point Proof was not.) At the issue price of $999, this was a prohibitively expensive option for most collectors, who instead chose the regular 1995-P Proof (available for a much more affordable $23). The set had a limit of 45,000, but not even that many were sold. By the time the sales period ended, only 30,125 sets had been purchased. In comparison, collectors bought nearly 440,000 of the 1995-P Proofs.

Hundreds of thousands of people collect Proof American Silver Eagles, and many desire to own a complete set—one coin of each date-and-mint combination. On the secondary market these collectors are forced to compete for a mere 30,125 available 1995-W coins. The law of supply and demand brings an inevitable result: even in raw (not professionally graded) form, these West Mint Proofs are worth a premium several times the issue price of $999 that originally paid for the entire set of 10th-anniversary coins.

The "king of American Silver Eagles" was ranked no. 4 in the *100 Greatest U.S. Modern Coins.* Authors Schechter and Garrett describe the rare bird: "The mystique and desirability of this coin have only grown over time. To say that the 1995-W is the 'key' to the series is an understatement. Its small mintage of 30,125 is dwarfed by that of every other Proof silver eagle in the series. Its value is nearly equal to that of all the other coins in the series combined. By any measure, the Proof silver eagle program is more popular today than at any point in the past, which only continues to bolster demand for its king rarity, the 1995-W."

On March 31, 2013, a PCGS Proof-70 Deep Cameo example sold for an astounding $86,654.70 in an online auction by Great Collections. At that time, PCGS had only graded a handful of examples in that grade but since the sale, more have been certified in this grade and prices have dropped substantially.

1995-W	<PF-65	PF-65	PF-66	PF-67	PF-68	PF-69	PF-70	Total
Certified	21	35	67	201	653	2,222	103	3,303
Value					$3,000	$5,000	$16,500	

1996, BULLION STRIKE

Mintage: 3,603,386

Minted at Philadelphia, without mintmark

Historical context: In May 1996 a monumental barrier was broken in the numismatic market: for the first time, a coin sold for more than $1 million at auction. It was the famous 1913 Liberty Head nickel from the Eliasberg Collection, and it went for $1,485,000. This was also the year that Congress passed legislation authorizing the U.S. Mint's State quarter program, which would launch in 1999.

The bullion price of silver ranged from about $4.70 to $5.80 through the year. Averaged against 1995, silver, like gold, held fairly steady. Gold's average price per ounce for the year was $389.09, compared to $385.50 for 1995.

1996 average silver price: $5.20/ounce.

Coin commentary: Demand for the American Silver Eagle reached a low in 1996. Because the coins are produced in quantities to satisfy public consumption, this low demand resulted in 1996 having the lowest bullion-strike mintage for the entire series. Today the coin enjoys a premium because of its relative scarcity.

A wise collector will carefully examine 1996 bullion strikes (especially those in unopened boxes) for small spots of white haze, called "milk spotting." This visually unpleasant effect is common enough on American Silver Eagles of the mid- to late 1990s that it pays to examine all specimens carefully: it will usually keep a coin from grading higher than MS-68.

The 1996 bullion strike was ranked no. 78 in the *100 Greatest U.S. Modern Coins*, third edition. This represented a drop of 11 points from the second edition. Authors Schechter and Garrett address the topic of milk spotting: "Concern regarding spotting dissuades dealers from bidding too aggressively on these issues and keeps their prices in check, despite their scarcity. This creates an opportunity for collectors who can take the extra time to search out a pristine example."

1996	<MS-65	MS-65	MS-66	MS-67	MS-68	MS-69	MS-70	Total
Certified	155	206	359	985	2,663	6,696	0	11,067
Value					$60	$85	$4,200	

1996-P, PROOF
Mintage: 500,000
Minted at Philadelphia, with P mintmark

Coin commentary: 1996 was the first year the ceiling for Proof American Silver Eagle production was reached. (Caps had been set, but never reached, for Proof mintages since 1990.) The maximum authorized mintage was 500,000 coins, and collectors and investors bought them up. Interestingly, demand for the bullion-strike American Silver Eagle reached an all-time low this same year.

The Proofs were sold by the Mint at an issue price of $23.

The Mint announced the sellout of the 1996-P Proof American Silver Eagle on May 13, 1997. "Sales of the half million Proof Silver Eagles mark the first sellout since the Mint established a maximum mintage for the coin in 1990," noted the press release, "and the highest Proof Silver Eagle sales since 1991's total sales of 511,950."

"The Proof Silver Eagle continues to be the world leader in silver coins," Mint Director Philip N. Diehl was quoted as saying. "Its classic design and affordability make this coin a unique value, both artistically and for collectors."

The press release continued as follows: "The Proof Silver Eagle obverse features Adolph A. Weinman's renowned 'Walking Liberty,' which originally appeared on the U.S. half dollar in 1916. Priced at $23, the Proof Silver Eagle went on sale on March 22, 1996."

1996-P	<PF-65	PF-65	PF-66	PF-67	PF-68	PF-69	PF-70	Total
Certified	9	8	33	68	444	8,702	1,508	10,772
Value					$75	$100	$350	

1997, BULLION STRIKE
Mintage: 4,295,004

Minted at Philadelphia, without mintmark

Historical context: The coin market continued to hum along in 1997, capped off by the sale of the amazing John J. Pittman collection, which was auctioned off starting this year. Pittman, who spent the majority of his career working as an executive at the Eastman Kodak Company, Rochester, New York, had an amazing talent for recognizing high-quality coins and good deals. He famously bought an 1833 $5 gold piece for $605. He also assembled an 1859 Proof set for less than $2,000—a set that later realized $387,500 at auction. Numismatist David Akers, who oversaw the sale of Pittman's collection, observed that while Pittman "was way ahead of his time in terms of knowing which coins to buy," he did so on a "definite budget."

In the summer of 1997 the American Numismatic Association urged people to check their pocket change for rare coins: to promote the hobby, the Association released 10 valuable coins, including four 1914-D Lincoln cents, into circulation in New York City.

For the most part, the precious-metals market was softer in 1997 than in 1996. Silver spiked in December to above $6 an ounce, but ended the year with an average price of $4.91, nearly 30 cents lower than the preceding year. Gold, too, was down, finishing the year with an average price of $332.39 an ounce—a far cry from the $389.09 average price a year earlier.

A new bullion program went into production in 1997. Joining the American Silver and Gold Eagle programs was a four-coin Platinum Eagle program, featuring a tenth-ounce $10 coin, a quarter-ounce $25 coin, a half-ounce $50 coin, and a one-ounce $100 coin. John Mercanti designed the coins' obverse, which depicts a close-up shot of the Statue of Liberty. Engraver Thomas D. Rogers provided a lovely soaring eagle design for the reverse, which "eagle-eyed" collectors may recognize as being remarkably similar to the eagle used for the reverse of the Sacagawea dollar. 173,850 bullion-strike platinum coins were sold in this, the series' inaugural year.

1997 average silver price: $4.91/ounce.

Coin commentary: The 1997 has the third-lowest mintage of the bullion-strike American Silver Eagles; premiums, however, are only modestly greater than those of others in the series. Although more than a thousand examples have been certified at MS-68 and lower, savvy collectors will seek a higher grade for their collections.

1997	<MS-65	MS-65	MS-66	MS-67	MS-68	MS-69	MS-70	Total
Certified	26	52	127	274	2,472	4,869	3	7,823
Value					$35	$50	$1,300	

1997-P, Proof

Mintage: 435,368

Minted at Philadelphia, with P mintmark

Coin commentary: Demand for the 1997-P Proof American Silver Eagle did not reach the authorized ceiling of 500,000 coins. Collectors purchased just over 435,000, giving this date the third-lowest mintage in the Proof series. In the secondary market the date commands a small premium over most others.

The Mint's issue price for a single Proof coin remained steady at $23, as it had since 1987.

The 1997-P Proof was also sold in the Mint's Impressions of Liberty set, which included the one-ounce gold bullion coin, the newly debuted one-ounce platinum coin, and the American Silver Eagle. Sales of the set reached the maximum authorized 5,000 sets (priced by the Mint at $1,499).

On January 15, 1998, the U.S. Mint announced that "approximately 7,000 of the 1997 Proof Silver American Eagle bullion coins remain in inventory from its 1997 production run of 435,000 coins, which ended December 31." The press release went on to quote Mint Director Philip N. Diehl as follows: "The mintage level for the 1997 Proof Silver Eagle will be the fourth lowest since the program began, so with only 7,000 remaining, we expect to sell all of these coins within the next month." The announcement concluded with a description of the coin: "Priced at $23, the Proof Silver Eagle obverse features Adolph A. Weinman's classic 'Walking Liberty,' which orginally appeared on the U.S. half dollar in 1916."

The number of 1997-P Proofs graded PF-70 has doubled since the publication of the second edition of this book in 2013—a good reminder that seemingly rare high grades can only become more common as time passes and more coins are submitted for professional grading and certification.

1997-P	<PF-65	PF-65	PF-66	PF-67	PF-68	PF-69	PF-70	Total
Certified	8	6	21	88	446	7,821	1,194	9,584
Value					$75	$95	$375	

1997 IMPRESSIONS OF LIBERTY SET

Mintage: 5,000

Minted at Philadelphia, without mintmarks

Set commentary: The U.S. Mint issued the limited-edition Impressions of Liberty Set to celebrate the debut of platinum in its lineup of bullion coins. The set included a one-ounce Proof American Gold Eagle, a one-ounce Proof American Platinum Eagle, and the Proof American Silver Eagle. Maximum production was set at 5,000 sets, and the price was $1,499. The issue sold out.

Packaging included a hardwood box and a certificate signed and numbered by Philip N. Diehl, director of the U.S. Mint.

The Mint announced the sellout of the 1997 Impressions of Liberty Set on June 27, 1997, only a few weeks after its June 6 debut. In its press release, the Mint noted that it had set a limit of one set per customer, "to ensure a fair chance for the maximum number of collectors to purchase the set."

"The great response to this new coinage removes any doubt about numismatic platinum coinage," said Mint Director Philip N. Diehl, "and augurs well for the launch of the bullion platinum Eagle this fall."

"The Impressions of Liberty Set was the first numbered set offered by the Mint," the press release continued, "and features one-ounce proof platinum, proof gold and proof silver American Eagles in a luxurious display case, including a certificate of authenticity personally signed by the director of the Mint. The obverse design of the .9995 Proof platinum coin is Mint sculptor/engraver John Mercanti's 'Portrait of Liberty,' and the reverse design is Mint sculptor/engraver Thomas D. Rogers Sr.'s 'Eagle Soaring Above America,' which will only appear on the coins this year. The one-ounce carries a $100 face value; the half-ounce a $50 face value; the quarter-ounce a $25 face value, and the tenth-ounce a $10 face value."

1997 Set	Proof
Value	$3,750

1998, BULLION STRIKE

Mintage: 4,847,549

Minted at Philadelphia, without mintmark

Historical context: The strength of the rare-coin market continued in 1998, with the sale of trophy rarities making headlines. The U.S. Mint issued various gold and silver commemorative coins, as it had in recent years. News made the rounds of the upcoming series of circulating commemorative coins (State quarters, to be issued through 2008) and a new dollar coin, the Sacagawea "golden dollar."

The year 1998 brought recognition to the U.S. Mint's commitment to customer service. On October 8, 1998, U.S. Senator Paul S. Sarbanes presented Mint Director Philip N. Diehl with a bronze Maryland Quality Award, honoring the work of the Mint's Customer Care Center. "This award is a testimony to the hard work and dedication of our staff at the Customer Care Center," said Diehl. "We have consistently demanded a higher and higher level of performance from our customer service team, and their commitment and results have been impressive." The award, presented at the 1998 Maryland Excellence Conference in Baltimore, recognized the Mint's significant gains toward achieving best-in-business customer service. A Mint press release noted that "The center now averages 90 percent of all orders delivered within three weeks, with overnight delivery provided on select items; 98 percent of orders requesting overnight delivery in 1997 were shipped within one day; and customer telephone inquiries are now answered within an average of six seconds, down from 50 seconds in 1996, and two minutes in 1995."

The average bullion price of silver rose by about 10 percent over the preceding year. Gold, meanwhile, was *down* at about the same rate, averaging $295.24 per ounce. Platinum fell about 6 percent, to $372.15.

1998 average silver price: $5.55/ounce.

Coin commentary: Consumer interest in silver increased in 1998 as the metal saw an early spike and ended the year about $0.65 higher than 1997. This interest translated into about 550,000 more bullion-strike American Silver Eagles being sold than the previous year.

1998	<MS-65	MS-65	MS-66	MS-67	MS-68	MS-69	MS-70	Total
Certified	35	35	123	316	1,121	4,286	17	5,933
Value					$30	$50	$1,200	

1998-P, Proof
Mintage: 450,000

Minted at Philadelphia, with P mintmark

Coin commentary: In 1998 the Mint raised its issue price for the Proof American Silver Eagle (the first increase since 1987), from $23 to $24 apiece. The coins went on sale March 27 and Mint Director Philip N. Diehl explained the upward price change, telling *Coin World* before the coins went on sale, ". . . . silver prices have risen in the past year, and given the fact we have not raised Proof silver Eagle prices in 12 years, we decided the time had come to do so." At the same time the maximum authorized mintage was lowered from 500,000 coins to 450,000. This resulted in a sellout despite the increased price.

More than 2,000 Proof 1998-P American Silver Eagles have been graded in PF-70, making it the least expensive date of the 1990s in that perfect grade. This quantity has doubled since the second edition of this book was published.

1998-P	<PF-65	PF-65	PF-66	PF-67	PF-68	PF-69	PF-70	Total
Certified	4	9	10	51	304	9,294	2,032	11,704
Value					$70	$90	$240	

1999, BULLION STRIKE
Mintage: 7,408,640

Minted at Philadelphia, without mintmark

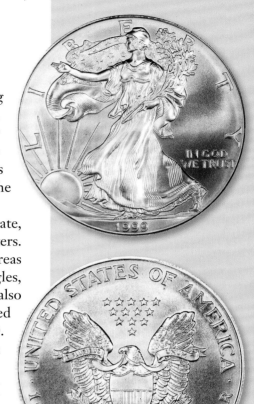

Historical context: The year 1999 saw renewed interest in coin collecting as the U.S. Mint launched the 50 State Quarters program. The program allowed states to choose their own designs, which were then adapted for coinage by skilled Mint engravers. State's designs were released at a rate of five per year by order of admission into the Union. The first five states (starting with Delaware) had begun the process of selecting their designs the previous year.

The release of each new quarter was cause for celebration in its home state, and untold millions of new collectors began to assemble sets of State quarters. The excitement generated by the program spilled over into several other areas of the hobby, including the sale of bullion-strike American Silver Eagles, which saw a significant increase in 1999. American Gold Eagle sales were also strong, largely due to hyped-up fears of mayhem as a result of an anticipated systemic computer failure when the clock hit midnight on January 1, 2000.

In total, 7,408,640 bullion-strike American Silver Eagles were issued in 1999, a 2.5 million coin increase over 1998, and the second-highest number of coins struck per release in the series up to this point, with only 1987's production run being higher.

Silver's bullion value decreased slightly in 1999, finishing the year at an average cost of $5.22 per ounce. Gold and platinum saw mixed results. Gold fell by $15, with an average price of $279.91 per ounce, and platinum was up $5 per ounce over its 1998 average, with an average price of $377.93.

1999 average silver price: $5.22/ounce.

Coin commentary: With such a substantial mintage, the 1999 bullion strike does not command significant premiums in raw (not professionally graded) form, or even in high Mint State grades up to MS-69. This issue is surprisingly rare certified in MS-70, with examples trading for substantial amounts at auction, e.g., one graded MS-70 by NGC sold for $17,625 at a June 2015 Heritage auction. Many examples of this issue are prone to spotting (see the related appendix).

On grading this issue, Scott Schechter, coauthor of *100 Greatest U.S. Modern Coins*, wrote in his "Making Moderns" column in the March 10, 2014, issue of *Coin World*, "The main concern among all the coins is milk spots. The spots form as a result of detergents used to wash the planchets. If inadequately rinsed away, the detergent is struck into the coin. Not apparent at first, over time it causes the coin's metal to discolor into an irregular milky-white haze or spots that cannot be removed. Not every coin is affected, but many produced during the middle and late 1990s are."

1999	<MS-65	MS-65	MS-66	MS-67	MS-68	MS-69	MS-70	Total
Certified	41	45	126	258	2,714	5,675	0	8,861
Value					$30	$50	$18,000	

1999-P, PROOF
Mintage: 549,769

Minted at Philadelphia, with P mintmark

Coin commentary: In 1999 the Mint continued with its issue price of $24 per coin for the Proof American Silver Eagle. The maximum authorized mintage was 550,000 and the issue sold out (the quantity of 549,769 accounts for record-keeping adjustments).

On April 21, 1999, the U.S. Mint announced the upcoming sale of the year's Proof Eagles, stating that it would begin sending out order forms on April 30.

Mint Director Philip N. Diehl was quoted as saying, "As the last Proof Eagles to be issued in the 1900s, we anticipate very high demand for these coins. To celebrate the coins' historical significance and to thank our customers for their loyalty, we're offering a specially commissioned Art Nouveau–style poster of the Augustus Saint-Gaudens 'Liberty' design free to those who place orders for $150 or more by June 15." The Mint's press release described the poster thus: "Renowned illustrator Oren Sherman has created a stunning Art Nouveau interpretation of the most cherished and enduring gold coin design on U.S. coinage, which originally graced the 1907 twenty-dollar gold piece. A nationally acclaimed artist and illustrator working in Boston's Fenway Studios, Sherman's award-winning poster designs have depicted the Tall Ships, the Kentucky Derby, the Brooklyn Bridge Centennial, the Ringling Brothers Barnum & Bailey Circus and numerous magazine covers, theatre productions, and movies."

With the vast majority of certified examples graded at PF-69 and PF-70, discerning collectors seek those higher grades rather than settling for a lower level. The number graded PF-70 has doubled since the second edition of this book was published.

1999-P	<PF-65	PF-65	PF-66	PF-67	PF-68	PF-69	PF-70	Total
Certified	9	7	19	78	430	8,535	1,463	10,541
Value					$60	$75	$300	

2000, BULLION STRIKE

Mintage: 9,239,132

Minted at West Point, without mintmark

Historical context: The nation's "dot com" investment bubble burst early in 2000, with many Internet-based and technology companies collapsing, being sold, or losing large parts of their market capitalization. (An extreme example: software firm The Learning Company, which Mattel bought in 1999 for $3.5 billion and sold in 2000 for $27.3 million.) The nation's general economy was strong, however, and unemployment was low. On the numismatic scene, the Sacagawea dollar debuted, and gold coins and ingots rescued from the wreck of the SS *Central America* were enthusiastically promoted. Interest in silver continued to be strong, resulting in a new post-1987 record for the American Silver Eagle's mintage.

Silver's average price for the year was down about 25 cents compared to 1999. Gold held steady, with its average price ($280.10 per ounce) a few cents higher than the preceding year. Platinum, meanwhile, saw a dramatic leap of more than $150 per ounce, from $377.93 to $544.03.

2000 average silver price: $4.95/ounce.

Coin commentary: Production of the 2000 American Silver Eagle exceeded 9.2 million coins, a high up to that point surpassed only by the 11.4 million minted in 1987. In spite of the millions produced and thousands professionally graded, only two coins have been certified by PCGS as perfect MS-70, resulting in a significant premium at that level.

Separately from its normal bullion-strike production, the U.S. Mint offered collectors a special "Millennium Coinage and Currency Set" that included three 2000-dated pieces of American money with the $1 denomination. These were the newly debuted Sacagawea golden dollar, the $1 Federal Reserve Note, and the American Silver Eagle. The set sold out with an authorized production limit of 75,000. American Silver Eagles from these sets are graded and slabbed by the professional third-party services with a "Millennium Set" designation.

2000	<MS-65	MS-65	MS-66	MS-67	MS-68	MS-69	MS-70	Total
Certified	51	109	281	1,066	5,126	14,227	12	20,872
Value					$30	$45	$4,400	

2000-P, PROOF
Mintage: 600,000

Minted at Philadelphia, with P mintmark

Coin commentary: The maximum mintage of the Proof American Silver Eagle was raised from 550,000 to 600,000 for the 2000-dated coin. The Mint's issue price remained at $24 per. Marketed as a collectible souvenir of "Y2K" (the year 2000), the Proof attracted enough demand to reach the production limit, and it sold out.

On May 9, 2000, John P. Mitchell, acting director of the U.S. Mint, made this observation about the Proof series as the American Silver Eagle rolled into the new millennium: "The 2000 American Eagle gold and silver Proof coins are the perfect collector's items to commemorate the year 2000. Renowned as classics of American design, the Proof Eagles rank among the most admired and sought after coins in the world."

The Mint's press release announcing the availability of the 2000 Proofs was enthusiastic. "Because mintages of the 2000 American Eagle Proof coins are limited, place your order early. . . . American Eagle Silver Proof coins are available for sale while quantities last or until the 2001 coins are issued. The Mint reserves the right to limit quantities and may discontinue accepting orders at any time."

2000-P	<PF-65	PF-65	PF-66	PF-67	PF-68	PF-69	PF-70	Total
Certified	9	9	38	90	666	10,933	1,410	13,155
Value					$65	$77	$400	

2001, BULLION STRIKE

Mintage: 9,001,711

Minted at West Point, without mintmark

Historical context: *Coin World*'s editor, Beth Deisher, on March 12, 2001, estimated that two million Americans were serious, active coin collectors, not including the millions of more casual collectors who were saving the Mint's popular new State quarters from circulation. Meanwhile the Sacagawea dollar, which had debuted in 2000, was rarely seen in pocket change; the coins were mainly stored in Treasury vaults, unwanted by the public. The U.S. Mint, after several years of increased coinage production, began to cut back and instigated a round of deep budget cuts and layoffs. The *Philadelphia Inquirer* described the situation in its December 2 edition ("Workers Suffer Following Production Frenzy at Philadelphia Mint; Excess Coinage Turns Into Job Cutbacks"): "It was only a year ago that the government was so frantic to make coins at the Philadelphia Mint it paid employees $100 weekly bonuses to work overtime. Workers practically needed a doctor's note to avoid putting in extra hours. . . . But now we're drowning in 2.4 billion pennies, 480 million nickels, 470 million dimes, 1.8 billion quarters, 62 million half-dollars, and 192 million Sacagawea golden dollars. That's the ocean of coinage—worth about $750 million—that has piled up in government vaults and armored-car coin terminals around the country since the summer of 2000. . . . [The] Mint curtailed production in April and has enacted deep employee and budget cutbacks in the last two months." The 2001 American Buffalo commemorative silver dollar sold out (500,000 coins total) and quickly commanded strong premiums on the secondary market. On the national scene, the September 11 terrorist attacks on American soil were the biggest news of the year.

Silver averaged down for the year, about 60 cents per ounce lower than 2000. Gold dropped about $8 per ounce, to $272.22. Platinum weakened but largely maintained its recent high level, averaging only $15 per ounce lower than the preceding year, at $529.04.

2001 average silver price: $4.38/ounce.

Coin commentary: Just over 9 million American Silver Eagles were minted in 2001—a small decline from the previous year but greater than any single year's mintage from the 1990s.

More than 28,000 bullion strikes of 2001 have been professionally graded by PCGS, including more than 3,800 in MS-68, more than 23,000 in MS-69, and a couple dozen in perfect PF-70.

PCGS certified 400 of the coins (all MS-69) in slabs with inserts autographed by road-racing cyclist Lance Armstrong. It also graded and authenticated 979 coins (all MS-69) certified as being found in a vault pulled from the Ground Zero devastation wrought on September 11, 2001.

2001	<MS-65	MS-65	MS-66	MS-67	MS-68	MS-69	MS-70	Total
Certified	20	21	60	214	3,884	24,252	31	28,487
Value					$30	$47	$900	

2001-W, PROOF
Mintage: 746,398
Minted at West Point, with W mintmark

Coin commentary: In 2001 production of the U.S. Mint's Proof American Silver Eagles was moved from the Philadelphia Mint to the West Point facility. The coins bear a W mintmark. Their issue price was maintained at $24, with sales commencing in mid-April, and there was enough collector interest that the production limit of 750,000 was reached.

The Mint announced the transition of Proof American Silver Eagle production to West Point on April 6, 2001. "As part of the Mint's commitment to continuous improvement," said Mint Director Jay W. Johnson, "we felt it was time to integrate and consolidate production of all the Proof American Eagle Coins at one facility. The entire family of Eagles—gold, platinum, and silver—will now be manufactured at the West Point Mint, where we're renovating and expanding our production facilities."

Associate Director for Numismatics David Pickens said, "The modernization program we're pursing will ensure continuous process improvement in the production of the highest-quality Proof precious-metals products. We're anticipating a great deal of interest in the 2001 W-mintmark Proof Silver Eagle, so we've raised the mintage level to 750,000 coins this year."

The Mint's press release noted the Mint's plans to continue striking Proof American Silver Eagles at West Point in the future. It went on to describe the coins: "Each 2001 American Eagle Proof coin is sealed in a protective capsule, comes in a presentation case, and is accompanied by an official certificate of authenticity, documenting the coin's place in history. The Mint will begin sending out order forms for the 2001 American Eagle Gold and Silver Proof Coins on April 18, 2001. Effective April 18, 9 a.m. (Eastern Time), these coins will be available for online orders at www.USMINT.gov."

The Proofs of 2001 are the earliest that can be acquired for less than $200 in perfect PF-70 condition.

The number graded PF-70 has doubled since publication of the second edition of this book.

2001-W	<PF-65	PF-65	PF-66	PF-67	PF-68	PF-69	PF-70	Total
Certified	9	11	26	91	525	17,160	2,414	20,236
Value					$65	$77	$120	

2002, BULLION STRIKE

Mintage: 10,539,026

Minted at West Point, without mintmark

Historical context: Numismatics once again entered the national spotlight with the record-setting sale of a 1933 double eagle ($20 gold coin) once owned by Egypt's King Farouk Al-Awwal. In order to allow for the sale of the coin, the U.S. government relented (but only slightly) on its stance that all 1933 double eagles were illegal to own since the coin was never monetized and released into circulation. Stack's and Sotheby's auctioned the coin. The winning bid came in at $7,590,000—plus $20 to cover its face value!

The sale capped off another good year for the hobby: the wildly successful 50 State Quarters program entered its fourth year, and sales of the bullion-strike American Silver Eagle soared past 10 million coins, finishing the year with a total mintage of 10,539,026—the second-highest total to date during the program's 16-year run.

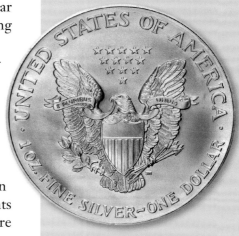

An editorial by Beth Deisher in *Coin World* quoted the U.S. Mint in stating that more than 139 million adults "have saved at least one of the 50 state quarters since the program was launched in January 1999." This led numismatic historian Q. David Bowers to observe, "Numismatics is expanding by leaps and bounds, with interest precipitated by television and shopping networks, Mint promotions, and more. Simply put, there are not enough old coins to go around. Recently when my fine friend David Sundman, CEO of Littleton Coin Company, visited, he stated that he would give an eyetooth to buy quantity lots of hundreds or thousands of large copper cents (1857 and earlier); these were once a commodity in the hobby, but now are usually seen only one at a time, even for common dates."

Silver prices saw a modest increase over 2001. Gold rose by nearly $40, averaging $311.33 per ounce. Platinum was up slightly, averaging $539.11 per ounce for the year.

2002 average silver price: $4.61/ounce.

Coin commentary: Increased demand for the American Silver Eagle led to a slight rise in the number of coins certified for collectors. Quality for this date is excellent, with nearly all pieces struck by the West Point Mint (uncredited on the coin) grading in the MS-68 to MS-69 range.

This issue is the last of the big-dollar regular-release top-pop coins in the series. To date, PCGS has graded 81 examples in MS-70. When these perfect coins come to market, demand sometimes pushes the price above $400.

2002	<MS-65	MS-65	MS-66	MS-67	MS-68	MS-69	MS-70	Total
Certified	15	21	43	192	1,941	13,470	81	15,764
Value					$30	$45	$150	

2002-W, Proof
Mintage: 647,342

Minted at West Point, with W mintmark

Coin commentary: In 2002, as in 2001, production of Proof American Silver Eagles was at the U.S. Mint's West Point facility, instead of Philadelphia or San Francisco, where nearly all pre-2001 Proofs had been struck. The coins bear West Point's W mintmark. Their official issue price was kept at $24. Sales began mid-year, on June 5, and a mintage limit of 750,000 was set. Collector demand was not sufficient for a sellout, although the 2002 sale of nearly 648,000 coins exceeded the mintages of most preceding years.

The Mint announced the upcoming sale of the 2002-W Proofs on May 22, 2002. Mint Director Henrietta Holsman Fore noted that the American Silver Eagle features one of the most popular obverse coin designs in history, "recalling the golden era of coinage during which the design was first produced. . . . The American Eagle Silver Proof coin features sculptor Adolph A. Weinman's 'Walking Liberty' design, depicting Liberty striding confidently toward a rising sun, first issued as the obverse of the half dollar in 1916." The Mint noted that "Each 2002 American Eagle Proof coin is sealed in a protective capsule, comes in a presentation case, and is accompanied by an official certificate of authenticity, documenting the coin's place in history."

2002-W	<PF-65	PF-65	PF-66	PF-67	PF-68	PF-69	PF-70	Total
Certified	9	7	17	40	299	9,688	2,510	12,570
Value					$60	$75	$120	

2003, BULLION STRIKE

Mintage: 8,495,008

Minted at West Point, without mintmark

Historical context: In March 2003, the United States and its allies launched an invasion of the nation of Iraq. Coalition forces, using an overwhelming complement of air and ground power, toppled the regime of Saddam Hussein within weeks. The war opened up a second theater of operations for the United States, with American involvement in Afghanistan continuing.

The wars, tax cuts, and general economic weakness pushed the federal budget deficit to a record $374 billion. On Wall Street, all three major indexes finished higher at the end of the year than they'd begun. The bear market took off after the market hit bottom in March. Bullion-strike American Silver Eagle sales, which started the year very strong, weakened in the bull market, finishing the year at a healthy but slightly disappointing mintage of 8,495,008.

The American Numismatic Association's spring National Money Show brought thousands of coin dealers and collectors to Charlotte, North Carolina, and the association's summer World's Fair of Money was held in Baltimore.

Silver's bullion price climbed through 2003, nearing the $6 per ounce mark in the fourth quarter and averaging slightly under $5 for the year—an increase of nearly 30 cents over 2002. Gold was more than $50 per ounce stronger, averaging $364.80 for the year; and platinum jumped more than $150 per ounce, to $691.31.

2003 average silver price: $4.87/ounce.

Coin commentary: The quality of the bullion-strike American Silver Eagles produced at West Point remained strong. Of the more than 18,000 coins submitted to PCGS for grading, more than 70% graded MS-69 or better. 719 examples earned the desirable MS-70 grade, a number that makes ownership of this coin at the "perfect" level doable, at less than $200 per coin.

PCGS has graded thousands of "First Strike" 2003 American Silver Eagles, about three fourths of which were given an MS-69 grade. Dozens of examples earned an MS-70, with one such piece selling for $1,600 in a September 2012 online auction. Since then, prices for perfect "First Strikes" have softened.

Collectors also had the opportunity to buy PCGS-certified bullion-strike American Silver Eagles in limited-edition holders featuring the signatures of such notable individuals as Private First Class Jessica Lynch (the first American POW successfully rescued since World War II), who signed 1,432 labels, and cycling legend Lance Armstrong, who signed 204. General Tommy Franks signed one.

2003	<MS-65	MS-65	MS-66	MS-67	MS-68	MS-69	MS-70	Total
Certified	10	22	49	136	2,139	15,077	719	18,151
Value					$30	$40	$150	

2003-W, PROOF
Mintage: 747,831

Minted at West Point, with W mintmark

Coin commentary: Proof sales were on a steady course in 2003: the Mint's issue price stayed at $24 per coin, and the mintage cap was 750,000 coins, as in previous years. Collector interest was up by about 100,000 coins—a general trend that would continue for several years—and the mintage neared but did not break the authorized limit.

On March 19, 2003, the U.S. Mint announced that the 2003-W Proofs would go on sale April 2. "For 17 years, the American Eagle Silver Proof coin has had special appeal to collectors," said Mint Director Henrietta Holsman Fore. "With almost 10 million coins sold since 1986, this classic American design has proven to be one of the most popular coins in our nation's history." The Mint's press release noted that the Proof coin would have a limited mintage of 750,000, would be minted at the West Point facility, and would bear the W mintmark. As in years past, the Mint's marketing materials extolled the beauty of the coin's artistry. "The American Eagle Silver coin's obverse (heads) design is Adolph A. Weinman's full-length figure of Liberty in full stride, enveloped in folds of the flag, with her right hand extended and branches of laurel and oak in her left. The reverse (tails) design, by United States Mint sculptor/engraver John Mercanti, features the heraldic eagle with shield, an olive branch in the right talon and arrows in the left." The Mint also emphasized the coin's attractive packaging: "Each 2003 American Eagle Silver Proof coin is sealed in a protective capsule, mounted in a handsome, satin-lined velvet presentation case, and accompanied by an official certificate of authenticity, documenting the coin's place in history." Finally, making sure consumers understood the importance of the program's urgency, the Mint advised: "Because mintages of the 2003 American Eagle Silver Proof coins are limited, orders should be placed early. American Eagle Silver Proof coins are available for sale while quantities last or until the 2004 coins are issued. The United States Mint reserves the right to limit quantities and may discontinue accepting orders at any time."

More than 10,000 of the 2003-W Proofs have been graded by PCGS—including more than 3,000 at the perfect PF-70 level. In addition, the firm encapsulated 103 coins (all PF-69) in "American Heroes Edition" packaging autographed by Jessica Lynch, an Army private rescued in Iraq (the first American POW rescued since World War II).

2003-W	<PF-65	PF-65	PF-66	PF-67	PF-68	PF-69	PF-70	Total
Certified	3	6	15	28	187	11,441	3,036	14,716
Value					$60	$75	$100	

2004, BULLION STRIKE

Mintage: 8,882,754

Minted at West Point, without mintmark

Historical context: In 2004 silver began a four-year increase in average annual price of $2 or more per ounce. Of course, 2004's average silver price of $6.67 an ounce doesn't tell the whole story: the metal started the year off strong before peaking in April at $8.29 per ounce. It took a dive in May (touching $5.50), but ended the year on a high note.

The resulting bull market saw mintages of bullion-strike American Silver Eagles rise to record levels. The mintage of the 2004 bullion strike rose to 8,882,754. Early sales of the coin were very strong, with production exceeding the one-million mark in January and February before finishing the year with more than 2.6 million coins struck.

The American Numismatic Association held its spring 2004 National Money Show in Portland, Oregon, and its larger annual summer show, the World's Fair of Money, in Pittsburgh. Also in 2004 the American Numismatic Society relocated its headquarters (including the Harry W. Bass Jr. Library, the ANS Museum and Library, and other facilities) to its own office building at 140 William Street in lower Manhattan, not far from where the Society was founded in 1858. The ANS would relocate again several years later to 75 Varick Street in lower Manhattan, where it remains today. In Maryland, in December, the annual Baltimore coin show was a huge success, with coordinators impressed by the convention's traffic of thousands of attendees.

By 2004, interest in the 50 State Quarters program had started to wane. The Wisconsin quarter caused a frenzy among variety collectors as several die-related varieties were discovered in coins minted in Denver.

2004 average silver price: $6.66/ounce.

Coin commentary: The typical coin submitted for professional grading is MS-69, which is indicative of the overall quality of coins struck this year by the West Point Mint. A number of beautifully toned coins have been certified, with grades ranging from MS-67 to MS-69. The purity of the .9993 fine silver can bring forth a captivating array of jewel-tone colors, and collectors pay strong premiums based on the pleasing nature and rich coloration of these naturally occurring toned coins.

Since the second edition of this book was published, the number of 2004 bullion strikes certified at MS-70 has more than tripled.

2004	<MS-65	MS-65	MS-66	MS-67	MS-68	MS-69	MS-70	Total
Certified	6	19	34	109	719	16,774	2,059	19,721
Value					$30	$40	$130	

2004-W, Proof

Mintage: 801,602

Minted at West Point, with W mintmark

Coin commentary: The Mint raised the maximum mintage for the 2004 American Silver Eagle Proof to 850,000 (up from a limit of 750,000 in 2003). At the same time it instituted a higher issue price—the first such increase since 1998. The price was raised from $24.00 to $27.95.

The Mint announced the upcoming sale of the 2004-W Proofs on April 20, 2004. "The American Eagle Silver Proof coin's obverse (heads) design is Adolph A. Weinman's full-length figure of Liberty in full stride with her right hand extended and branches of laurel and oak in her left," the press materials noted. "The reverse (tails) design, by United States Mint sculptor/engraver John Mercanti, features the heraldic eagle with shield, an olive branch in the right talon, and arrows in the left. Each 2004 American Eagle Silver Proof coin is sealed in a protective capsule; mounted in a handsome, satin-lined velvet presentation case; and accompanied by a certificate of authenticity documenting the coin's place in history. Because mintages of the 2004 American Eagle Silver Proof coins are limited, orders should be placed early. American Eagle Silver Proof coins are available for sale while quantities last or until the 2005 coins are issued. The United States Mint reserves the right to limit quantities and may discontinue accepting orders at any time."

The third-party grading services have certified thousands of Proofs of 2004, most of them at the PF-69 level, but many in PF-70. Since the second edition of this book was published, the quantity certified as PF-70 has more than doubled. The coin is affordable even in the latter perfect grade—among the least expensive of the entire series.

2004-W	<PF-65	PF-65	PF-66	PF-67	PF-68	PF-69	PF-70	Total
Certified	3	3	11	23	151	10,887	3,646	14,724
Value					$65	$77	$90	

2005, BULLION STRIKE

Mintage: 8,891,025

Minted at West Point, without mintmark

Historical context: The first year of President George W. Bush's second term proved to be a time of great challenge for the American people. Hurricane Katrina struck the Gulf Coast in late August, wreaking devastation on an epic scale. The federal government famously mishandled the disaster, and fuel prices soared. Stocks finished the year slightly higher than they had started.

In numismatics, 2005 was a record year for the sale of ultra-rarities, with 14 coins bringing $1 million or more each (a mark first surpassed only nine years earlier). Notable pieces include a 1787 Brasher doubloon (Punch on Breast variety), and a 1907 Ultra High Relief, Lettered Edge, 1907 Saint-Gaudens double eagle. Both sold for $2.99 million.

The Colorado-based American Numismatic Association boasted membership of more than 32,000 hobby enthusiasts in 2005. The Association held its spring National Money Show in Kansas City, and, in the summer, the ANA World's Fair of Money attracted coin collectors, investors, and dealers to San Francisco. That December the ANA named its museum after hobby legend Edward C. Rochette—a former ANA president, executive director, and editor of *The Numismatist*. Rochette had also been instrumental in the founding of the ANA's annual Summer Seminars, held at Association headquarters in Colorado Springs.

Silver continued its rise. Gold, too, had a good year, with an average price of $446, which was an increase of $40 over 2004's average price. Platinum rose in price by $50, finishing at an average price per ounce of $896.87.

2005 average silver price: $8.82/ounce.

Coin commentary: 2005 marked the debut of PCGS's "First Strike" program, a designation called "Early Release" by NGC. Coins submitted for these designations from preceding years had to be submitted in their original government-shipping packaging, unopened, with a postmark from within 30 days of their release. This accounts for the low numbers of pre-2004 "First Strike" and "Early Release" coins compared to the population of such coins of 2005.

There is a market for First Strike and Early Release coins, and coins encapsulated with special labels, though many professional numismatists such as Q. David Bowers advise collectors to "buy the coin and not the slab." In *American Gold and Silver*, this advice is summarized in the appendix on investing: "This kind of special packaging has limited premium value over the long run, in the secondary marketplace. A slab autographed by a coin designer or other famous person might have personal sentimental value, but ask yourself if other collectors will pay a premium for it in the future, and let your own buying be guided by the answer. Usually coin collectors consider only the alphanumeric certified grade (MS-69, PF-70, and the like) and pay little or no premium for extra adjectives."

2005	<MS-65	MS-65	MS-66	MS-67	MS-68	MS-69	MS-70	Total
Certified	11	24	52	161	648	51,664	1,752	54,312
Value					$25	$30	$100	

2005-W, PROOF

Mintage: 816,663

Minted at West Point, with W mintmark

Coin commentary: In 2005 the U.S. Mint started selling its Proof American Silver Eagles earlier in the year than normal (March 15, compared to April or even as late as May or June in recent years). The Mint kept the issue price at $27.95 after having raised it the year before. It also abolished the Proof coins' mintage limit, which had already been raised several times. Proof sales for 2005 were the highest since 1986 and 1987, the first two years of the bullion program. Collectors purchased more than 816,000 of the 2005-W coins.

On March 10, 2005, the U.S. Mint announced that the 2005-W American Silver Eagle Proof coins "will be available for sale on March 15, 2005, at 12:00 noon (ET). The release date for this product is six weeks earlier than in 2004, as part of the United States Mint's commitment to make many of its 2005 products available earlier in the year." The official press release went on to describe the issue: "Priced at $27.95 each, the 2005 American Eagle Silver Proof coins have an unlimited mintage and are minted at the United States Mint at West Point. The coins bear the 'W' mintmark. The popularity of the Silver Eagle Proof program has been increasing steadily over the past few years, and the United States Mint is committed to meeting the collecting needs of its longtime customers, as well as accommodating the requirements of the many new coin collectors joining the ranks of this growing hobby." The Mint's special care in packaging the Proofs was emphasized in its announcement: "Each 2005 American Eagle Silver Proof coin is sealed in a protective capsule; mounted in a handsome, satin-lined velvet presentation case; and accompanied by a certificate of authenticity documenting the coin's place in history." The Mint also noted a service for coin collectors: "As an added convenience, customers can participate in a subscription-ordering program in which American Eagle Silver Proof coins can be charged and shipped to the customer automatically as each new coin is released."

PCGS and NGC have certified thousands of Proofs of 2005, most of them at the PF-69 level, but a considerable quantity (more than 4,000 by PCGS) in PF-70. The 2005-W is affordable even in the latter perfect grade—among the least expensive of the entire series.

2005-W	<PF-65	PF-65	PF-66	PF-67	PF-68	PF-69	PF-70	Total
Certified	0	5	10	8	106	17,259	4,032	21,420
Value					$60	$75	$95	

2006, BULLION STRIKE

Mintage: 10,676,522

Minted at West Point, without mintmark

Historical context: The price of silver jumped from an average of $8.82 an ounce to $11.54 in 2006. For the second time in five years, mintages of bullion-strike American Silver Eagles eclipsed the 10 million mark. Stocks continued to perform well, despite a slowing real-estate market. Housing prices peaked in 2006, while the number of foreclosures exceeded 1.2 million for the first time in United States history.

The U.S. coin market was strong through the middle of the year, when the weakening economy began to affect it. The U.S. Mint expanded the American Silver Eagle program for the first time in its 20-year history, offering not just bullion-strike and Proof versions of the coin, but also a specially prepared burnished version bearing the W mintmark for West Point. Not only that, but a Reverse Proof featuring frosted fields and mirrored devices was produced for the first time ever in the Mint's history.

The numismatic press updated the hobby community on John Mercanti's elevation to chief engraver at the U.S. Mint in 2006. *Numismatic News* reported on June 13: "Mercanti's responsibilities will include overseeing the artistic design of all new products; the complete development of master tooling (including the reduction hub, master die and work hubs), from approved designs through approved trial strikes; supervision of tool makers, engravers, and other craft and trades personnel involved in the development of master tooling; and the timely delivery of reduction hubs/master dies for all recurring and new products to the die shops at the mints in Denver and Philadelphia." *Coin World* in a June 12 article reported that "The demands on the engraving staff today include projects that in the early stages of Mercanti's career would have been granted many months of preparation time, but now have deadlines of just weeks after inception. The workload has nearly tripled over the past few years, and is only expected to increase."

2006 average silver price: $11.54/ounce.

Coin commentary: West Point again had the honor of minting the American Silver Eagle bullion strikes in 2006. Consistent with their typical production quality, coins of this date were beautifully struck on high-quality planchets. The typical coin is virtually flawless with a beautiful lightly-satin finish.

As general demand for the American Silver Eagle increased, so did collector demand for certified examples. PCGS and NGC have graded hundreds of thousands of the 2006 bullion strike, including many tens of thousands designated as First Strike or Early Release. The vast majority grade MS-69.

Collectors seeking slabbed perfect-grade MS-70 coins have ample opportunity to take their pick from among thousands that have earned that grade from PCGS and NGC, including many hundreds labeled as First Strike or Early Release.

2006	<MS-65	MS-65	MS-66	MS-67	MS-68	MS-69	MS-70	Total
Certified	2	13	41	129	328	148,043	1,562	150,118
Value					$25	$30	$95	

2006-W, BURNISHED

Mintage: 468,020

Minted at West Point, with W mintmark

Coin commentary: The Burnished (called *Uncirculated* by the Mint) 2006-W American Silver Eagle was released late in the year. In celebration of the 20th anniversary of the Mint's bullion coinage program, the W mintmark was used on these special bullion coins made at West Point. The coins were struck on what the Mint called "burnished" planchets. Some of these 2006-W Burnished American Silver Eagles were packaged for collectors in three-coin 20th Anniversary sets (along with a Proof and Reverse Proof coin; see page 93 for more on those sets). In addition to being available in sets, these American Silver Eagles were offered individually, with an issue price of $19.95 per coin (a price between that of the regular bullion-strike coin and the Proof version).

The finish of the Burnished coin is nearly indistinguishable from that of the regular bullion issue.

The 2006-W Burnished American Silver Eagle is ranked no. 64 among the *100 Greatest U.S. Modern Coins*.

Also see page 94 for more information on a 20th Anniversary gold-and-silver two-coin set (which included a Burnished 2006-W American Silver Eagle) issued in 2006.

2006-W, Burnished	<MS-65	MS-65	MS-66	MS-67	MS-68	MS-69	MS-70	Total
Certified	4	13	56	150	2,177	24,682	3,698	30,780
Value					$55	$65	$120	

2006-W, Proof

Mintage: 1,092,477

Minted at West Point, with W mintmark

Coin commentary: The 2006-W Proof was issued by the Mint early in the year. There was no production limit established for the mintage of this collectible coin. It was released at an issue price of $27.95 per coin (the same price as in recent years). Collector demand for this year's Proof coin exceeded 1 million for the first time since the American Silver Eagle debuted in 1986.

Sales of the 2006-W Proof were boosted by the coin's inclusion in the 20th Anniversary Silver Eagle Set, which went on sale August 30, 2006, and which ultimately accounted for nearly 250,000 of the total Proof coins sold. For more information on the anniversary set, see page 93.

The U.S. Mint announced on April 5, 2006, that the year's Proof American Silver Eagles would be available at the Mint's booth at the American Numismatic Association's National Money Show, April 7 through 9. The show was held at the Cobb Galleria Centre in Atlanta, Georgia.

In *Coin World*, Steve Roach used the 2006-W Proof as an example in an article about First Strike coins. "By virtue of population numbers alone, early release coins generally are not scarcer than their later-issued brethren," he noted. "Take for example the Proof 2006-W American Eagle silver dollar. As of mid-June, PCGS graded 7,285 examples under its normal program and 7,716 pieces under its First Strike program. The early release programs take into account only when a coin was shipped from the U.S. Mint, not when it was minted. The programs were first developed by the grading services in 2005. The 'First Strikes' are visually imperceptible from their later-released counterparts" (*Coin World*, "First Strikes, Early Releases: Buyers Should Do Homework," August 1, 2011).

PCGS and NGC have graded tens of thousands of the 2006-W Proof, most in PF-69 but a significant percentage of them in PF-70, making even the most "perfect" coins affordable.

2006-W, Proof	<PF-65	PF-65	PF-66	PF-67	PF-68	PF-69	PF-70	Total
Certified	4	10	19	76	715	30,042	9,170	40,036
Value					$65	$75	$100	

2006-P, Reverse Proof
Mintage: 248,875

Minted at Philadelphia, with P mintmark

Coin commentary: The 2006-P Reverse Proof American Silver Eagle was sold by the U.S. Mint in a special three-coin 20th Anniversary Silver Eagle set. This set, announced on August 21 of that year and available for purchase on August 30, was the only way of acquiring the Reverse Proof coin. Mintage was capped at 250,000 sets, with a limit of 10 sets per household. The issue price for the set was $100.

This was the first time the Mint used a Reverse Proof format on the American Silver Eagle. Mint literature described the effect as "a unique finish which results in a frosted field, or background, and a brilliant, mirror-like finish on the raised elements of the coin, including the design and inscriptions."

Collector interest was high from the first hour of sales, and the anniversary sets sold out in a little more than two months. Weeks out of the gate they were being traded on the secondary market at twice their issue price.

The coin is ranked no. 32 among the *100 Greatest U.S. Modern Coins.* "Its look is so distinctive within the series that the Reverse Proof will always be a curious standout among silver eagles," write Schechter and Garrett.

The 2006-P Reverse Proof American Silver Eagle, like many of the series' recent special-finish collectibles, has been discussed in the trade papers. Market observer Eric Jordan noted in an August 2012 commentary in *Numismatic News* that the 2006-P is no longer the only Reverse Proof in the series, but it still holds appeal for collectors. "The distinction of being the only one is gone," wrote Jordan, "but something else is taking its place and what that will be is largely dependent on how these sets are going to be put together. . . . [If collectors] start working on sets of Reverse Proofs as a cost-effective way to get around buying an expensive 1995-W, then this 2006-P and by extension its Reverse Proof siblings may get a life of their own" (*Numismatic News,* "Silver Eagle: The Modern Morgan," August 21, 2012).

2006-P, Reverse Proof	<PF-65	PF-65	PF-66	PF-67	PF-68	PF-69	PF-70	Total
Certified	6	7	15	88	1,658	17,786	3,701	23,261
Value					$170	$200	$320	

2006 AMERICAN EAGLE
20TH ANNIVERSARY SILVER COIN SET
Mintage: 248,875
Minted at West Point and Philadelphia, with W and P mintmarks

Set commentary: This set of coins marked the 20th anniversary of the United States' bullion program with three American Silver Eagles, each produced with a different finish. One had the Mint's new Burnished (*Uncirculated*, in Mint jargon) finish; another had the standard brilliant mirror-like Proof finish; and another had the Reverse Proof finish (used on the American Silver Eagle for the first time).

The set went on sale August 30, 2006, at the issue price of $100, and with a production limit of 250,000 sets. The Mint sought to curb speculation and hoarding by limiting each household to 10 sets. Collectors and investors were excited about the set, its innovative finish formats, its historical significance, and its limited mintage. The issue sold out in about 10 weeks, and by that time prices were rising on the secondary market. The set was selling for six times its issue price by mid-2007, after which its value sloped down and leveled out.

See each coin's separate listing for more information.

2006 Set	
Value	$425

2006-W AMERICAN EAGLE 20TH ANNIVERSARY GOLD & SILVER COIN SET

Mintage: 20,000

Minted at West Point, with W mintmarks

Set commentary: The U.S. Mint in 2006 issued a 20th Anniversary Gold and Silver Set, marking this milestone in the nation's bullion coinage program. Each set contains a one-ounce American Gold Eagle and an American Silver Eagle. The coins bear the W mintmark of the West Point facility and were struck in the Burnished or "Uncirculated" finish.

Production of the two-coin set was limited to 20,000. It was packaged with an informative booklet outlining the international history of gold and silver coins. The issue price was $850, with a limit of 10 sets per household, and there was enough collector and investor interest to cause a sellout.

2006-W Set	Unc
Value	$1,860

2007, Bullion Strike
Mintage: 9,028,036

Minted at West Point, without mintmark

Historical context: The Dow-Jones Industrial Average surpassed 14,000 for the first time in July 2007. Interest rates were high and the real-estate market was weakening. In the numismatic market, higher interest rates and slow sales translated into a scarcity of ready cash for many coin dealers. A strong market existed for classic collector coins—key dates in popular series—as well as for higher-grade silver and gold coins. Exonumia (medals and tokens) and paper currency also enjoyed robust markets.

In an attempt to reinvigorate the "golden" dollar coin program, Congress authorized the release of a new series of dollars featuring the likenesses of the presidents of the United States. The program also called for the continued production of a Native American dollar coin featuring a modified Sacagawea obverse and new reverses celebrating Native American heritage.

The new dollar coins were eagerly awaited by collectors. Production errors unintentionally left the congressionally mandated edge lettering off of some coins. These coins became the first U.S. coins struck in more than a hundred years to omit the motto IN GOD WE TRUST. These accidental varieties became known as "Godless dollars."

The *Philadelphia Inquirer* described the new small-size dollars as "cool" and "edgy" (playing off their innovative edge lettering). "Hold up one of the new dollar coins, which debuted two days ago, and you'll see letters and numbers around the rim," the *Inquirer* reported ("New Dollar Coins Rolled Out," February 17, 2007). "The P, of course, is for the Philadelphia Mint, the world's biggest. Other features to inspire interest and acceptance: a big '$1' on the back (other coins spell out amounts). Presidents on the front, a new one every three months. The Statue of Liberty on the back. . . . Time will tell whether the coins become common in pockets and cash registers. The Mint has dreams: 'I even suspect the tooth fairy will love leaving these beautiful coins under pillows,' Washington-based director Edmund C. Moy stated."

Silver as bullion continued on the rise, its average increasing by about $1.75 per ounce over 2006. Gold's average rose as well, climbing nearly $100 per ounce, to $699.00, and platinum saw another healthy increase of $160, averaging at $1,303.05 for the year.

2007 average silver price: $13.32/ounce.

Coin commentary: Demand dropped slightly for the American Silver Eagle in 2007, compared to 2006. They remain among the series' most affordable.

2007	<MS-65	MS-65	MS-66	MS-67	MS-68	MS-69	MS-70	Total
Certified	2	11	39	78	188	18,912	1,091	20,321
Value					$30	$35	$50	

2007-W, BURNISHED

Mintage: 621,333

Minted at West Point, with W mintmark

Coin commentary: In 2007 the U.S. Mint released its second Burnished (or *Uncirculated*) American Silver Eagle. Like the Burnished issue of the previous year, the 2007-W was produced at West Point and bears that facility's unique mintmark. Sold directly to the public, its issue price was $21.95 per coin—an increase of $2 over 2006—and no mintage limit was mandated. Collector interest pushed the mintage to more than 150,000 coins over the quantity sold in 2006.

In addition to being offered individually, the 2007-W Burnished American Silver Eagle was packaged in the 2007 U.S. Mint Annual Uncirculated Dollar Coin Set (along with Satin finish strikes of the year's Sacagawea dollar and four Presidential dollars). The set's issue price was $31.95.

PCGS and NGC have graded tens of thousands of the 2007-W Burnished American Silver Eagles. Most of these are MS-69, but a significant quantity of thousands are MS-70. Collectors seeking perfection do not have to pay a large premium.

2007-W, Burnished	<MS-65	MS-65	MS-66	MS-67	MS-68	MS-69	MS-70	Total
Certified	0	0	8	78	228	30,977	8,211	39,502
Value					$36	$50	$65	

2007-W, Proof

Mintage: 821,759

Minted at West Point, with W mintmark

Coin commentary: The 2007-W Proof American Silver Eagle was issued by the Mint on March 27 of that year. There was no maximum mandated for the production of this collectible release. It was issued at $29.95 per coin—an increase of $2 over the 2006 price. Perhaps as a result, collector demand declined compared to the previous year, by more than 270,000 coins.

The Mint announced the upcoming sale of the 2007 Proof coins in a press release dated March 12, 2007. "Priced at $29.95 each, the 2007 American Eagle Silver Proof coins will not have a pre-determined mintage," the letter stated, "as the United States Mint will produce these coins to meet demand. The American Eagle Silver Coins are minted at the United States Mint at West Point, with the 'W' mintmark."

Describing the coin, the Mint's promotional materials noted that "The American Eagle Silver Proof coin's obverse (heads) design is Adolph A. Weinman's full-length figure of Liberty in full stride with her right hand extended and branches of laurel and oak in her left. The reverse (tails) design, by United States Mint Sculptor-Engraver John Mercanti, features the heraldic eagle with shield, an olive branch in the right talon and arrows in the left."

The Mint lavished praise on the coins' attractive packaging: "Each 2007 American Eagle Silver Proof coin is sealed in a protective capsule; mounted in a handsome, satin-lined velvet presentation case; and accompanied by a certificate of authenticity documenting the coin's place in history."

Tens of thousands of 2007-W Proofs have been professionally graded by NGC and PCGS. Historically some 25 percent of this quantity has graded at the PF-70 level, with the bulk of the remainder being PF-69. This reflects the high quality that characterizes modern U.S. Mint production. Anything below PF-69 is, ironically, a "condition rarity"—not that collectors would pay a premium for that rare distinction.

2007-W, Proof	<PF-65	PF-65	PF-66	PF-67	PF-68	PF-69	PF-70	Total
Certified	3	5	7	35	157	14,442	4,200	18,849
Value					$60	$65	$70	

2008, BULLION STRIKE

Mintage: 20,583,000

Minted at West Point, without mintmark

Historical context: Three stories dominated the news in 2008: the nation's worsening financial crisis (in particular the collapse of the housing market); the presidential campaign of Republican John McCain vs. Democrat Barack Obama; and Obama's election that November. In numismatics, the market for high-quality coins maintained its strength, although collector spending was slowing down slightly.

Demand for silver surged worldwide in the first half of the year, with its price spiking upward of $20 per ounce but settling back in the second half; its yearly average increased over 2007 by more than $1.50 per ounce. Gold saw a dramatic bump, from $699 per ounce in 2007 to an average of $900 in 2008. Platinum also climbed, up $270 per ounce to $1,573.53.

2008 average silver price: $14.99/ounce.

Coin commentary: Demand for the American Silver Eagle exploded in 2008, with production more than doubling the previous year's output. The mintage of 20.6 million coins was far greater than the previous record, set in 1987, of 11.4 million. The Mint struggled to keep up with production, and had to temporarily suspend (and then ration) orders for the coin. It even stopped orders for the Proof version, diverting all silver blanks to production of the regular bullion strikes.

The Mint issued a statement (reported in the June 5, 2008, issue of *Numismatic News*): "Since the introduction of the 2008 American Eagle Silver Bullion Coin Program, the United States Mint has issued a record number of coins (about 9.65 million), as demand for them has increased exponentially. That number is almost as high as . . . production for the entire year of 2007 (about 9.8 million). By law, the . . . bullion coins must meet exacting specifications and must be composed of newly mined silver acquired from domestic sources. The United States Mint will continue to make every effort to increase its acquisition of silver bullion blanks that meet these specifications and requirements to address continuing high demand in the silver bullion coin market." Production did continue, with millions more of the coins being minted through the year.

With so many 2008 bullion strikes in existence, the coin is one of the most affordable of the series.

2008	<MS-65	MS-65	MS-66	MS-67	MS-68	MS-69	MS-70	Total
Certified	2	9	19	79	58,625	304,311	12,335	375,380
Value					$27	$29	$50	

2008-W, BURNISHED

Mintage: 533,757

Minted at West Point, with W mintmark

Coin commentary: In 2008 the U.S. Mint produced its third Burnished (or *Uncirculated*) American Silver Eagle. Like the Burnished issue of previous years, the coin was struck at West Point and bears that facility's W mintmark. Sold directly to the public, its issue price was $25.95 per coin and no mintage limit was set. Collector interest was down by about 90,000 coins, compared to 2007.

The Mint waxed poetic in its March 10, 2008, announcement of the coin's release. "'She walks in beauty, like the night / Of cloudless climes and starry skies.' Although Lord Byron wrote those words almost two centuries ago, they can serve to describe the classic beauty of Adolph Weinman's image of Liberty. That image—featured on United States Mint American Eagle bullion and Proof coins since 1986—graces the 2008 American Eagle Silver Uncirculated coin, scheduled for release on March 17 at noon." The Mint's promotional materials went on to further describe the coin's design and its packaging: "The 2008 American Eagle Silver Uncirculated coin, offered at $25.95, contains one troy ounce of .999 silver. The obverse features Liberty in full stride enveloped in the folds of the American flag, with her right hand extended and branches of laurel and oak in her left. Featured on the coin's reverse is the image of a heraldic eagle with shield, an olive branch in the right talon and arrows in the left. Struck on specially burnished blanks, the American Eagle Uncirculated coins feature a finish similar to their bullion counterparts, but carry the 'W' mintmark, indicating their production at the United States mint at West Point. Each coin is encapsulated in protective plastic and placed in a blue presentation case accompanied by a certificate of authenticity signed by the director of the United States Mint, Edmund C. Moy."

In addition to being offered individually, the 2008-W Burnished American Silver Eagle was packaged in the 2008 U.S. Mint Annual Uncirculated Dollar Coin Set (along with Satin finish strikes of the year's Sacagawea dollar and four Presidential dollars). The set's issue price was $37.95.

Substantial quantities have been graded MS-70.

2008-W, Burnished	<MS-65	MS-65	MS-66	MS-67	MS-68	MS-69	MS-70	Total
Certified	0	0	2	5	47	11,556	4,374	15,994
Value					$40	$50	$80	

2008-W, BURNISHED, REVERSE OF 2007

Mintage: *47,000 (estimated)*

Minted at West Point, with W mintmark

Coin commentary: The 2008-W, Reverse of 2007, Burnished American Silver Eagle is the only significant die variety in the series. Since its discovery in mid-April 2008 it has excited collectors and has been avidly sought as a required coin in the set.

The variety is the result of rehubbing (creation of a new hub, which is used to make coinage dies) during the Mint's transition to digital engraving methods. Minor changes for the new 2008 coins were made to the design of the reverse, most notably in the font used in the legends. The font difference is most noticeable in the U of UNITED. In the lettering style of 1986–2007, the U has a smooth curve at the bottom right. In the new lettering style adopted for 2008, the U has a spur or foot at the bottom right.

The Reverse of 2007 variety is ranked no. 17 in the book *100 Greatest U.S. Modern Coins*, which describes the Mint's reaction to the coin's discovery. "The Mint responded quickly, acknowledging that during three production shifts for the 2008 coins, dies originally crafted for 2007-W silver eagle production were used inadvertently. Approximately 47,000 silver eagles had been struck with the reverse style of 2007. This type of variety is called *transitional* because it is a hybrid that combines the styles of coins used in two consecutive years."

2008-W, Burnished, Reverse of 2007	<MS-65	MS-65	MS-66	MS-67	MS-68	MS-69	MS-70	Total
Certified	0	1	1	11	63	3,808	636	4,523
Value					$400	$450	$1,000	

2008-W, PROOF
Mintage: 700,979

Minted at West Point, with W mintmark

Coin commentary: The hyperactive silver market of 2008 adversely affected production of the year's Proof American Silver Eagle. As in recent years, no maximum mintage limit was established for the Proof coins; however, by August of 2008 the Mint was forced to suspend sales of the Proofs because of a shortage of silver blanks. All available and incoming silver planchets were being diverted from the Proof coinage to continue production of regular bullion strikes. (The American Silver Eagle's authorizing legislation mandates that the bullion coins be minted "in quantities sufficient to meet public demand," while the Treasury Department has discretion over how many collector-format coins, such as Proofs, are struck.)

Sale of the Proof coins was suspended in mid-August, and the coin was listed as "Not Available" in the Mint's online catalog. The "temporary" suspension was not lifted, so production of 2008-W Proofs effectively ended after about 700,000 of the coins were sold. The suspension of Proof coinage continued through 2009, and it wasn't until 2010 that the collector-format coins were produced again.

The 2008-W Proof had an issue price of $31.95.

Historically, the thousands of 2008-W Proofs professionally graded by NGC and PCGS have yielded about 25 percent in PF-70, making perfect coins readily available and affordable.

2008-W, Proof	<PF-65	PF-65	PF-66	PF-67	PF-68	PF-69	PF-70	Total
Certified	2	7	6	18	124	13,793	5,079	19,029
Value					$65	$75	$100	

101

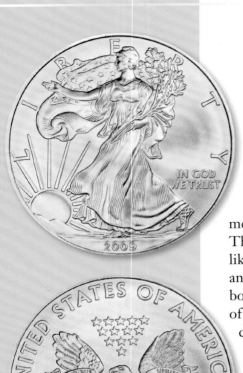

2009, BULLION STRIKE

Mintage: 30,459,000

Minted at West Point, without mintmark

Historical context: The American economy, in turmoil for most of 2009, hit rock bottom but by the end of the year began to show some signs of improvement. In numismatics, retail prices held steady for most series. However, overall retail and auction sales volume was slightly less than in recent years.

This year marked the bicentennial of the birth of Abraham Lincoln, commemorated by the U.S. Mint in four new reverse designs for the Lincoln cent. The first, Birth and Early Childhood in Kentucky, depicts a small log cabin like the one in which Lincoln was born. The second, Formative Years in Indiana, shows a youthful Abe Lincoln taking a break from rail-splitting to read a book. On the third coin, Professional Life in Illinois, Lincoln stands in front of the state capitol of Illinois (the design commemorates his pre-presidential career in law and politics). Finally, Presidency in Washington depicts the partially completed U.S. Capitol dome as it appeared when Lincoln held office. The state of the Capitol building represents "the unfinished business of a nation torn apart by slavery and the Civil War."

Silver saw swings in its bullion value, ranging from $10.51 to just over $19 per ounce. Its average for the year was about 30 cents lower than 2008's. Interest in gold was intense, with its price peaking at $1,215 per ounce in December, but its overall average for the year was up a mere 1 percent (compared to 2008), to $910 per ounce. Platinum tumbled $370, to $1,203.49.

2009 average silver price: $14.66/ounce.

Coin commentary: In a repeat of 2008, in 2009 demand for the American Silver Eagle made the coin's mintage skyrocket. The supply of silver continued to be a production challenge for the Mint. As in the previous year, the Mint rationed purchase of the bullion coins, with its authorized distributors limited to preset quantities. To further assist production, all silver blanks in 2009 were reserved for standard bullion-strike coins, with none allocated for Proofs or Burnished pieces. The distributor rationing was lifted on June 15 after the Mint's silver-planchet suppliers were able to meet demand; but by late November it had to temporarily *suspend* sales, and then re-establish the rationing system.

Even with these challenges, the Mint produced more than 30 million American Silver Eagles by year's end, setting another record for the series.

Of the hundreds of thousands of 2009 bullion strikes professionally graded by NGC and PCGS, nearly half were granted the Early Release or First Strike designation.

2009	<MS-65	MS-65	MS-66	MS-67	MS-68	MS-69	MS-70	Total
Certified	3	14	26	69	123,757	117,460	40,519	281,848
Value					$25	$30	$60	

2010, BULLION STRIKE

Mintage: 34,764,500

Minted at West Point, without mintmark

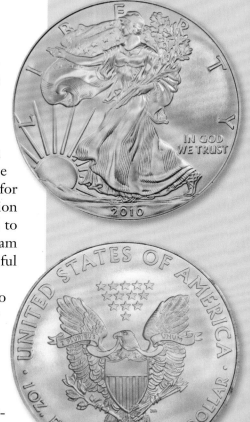

Historical context: The year 2010 started with a catastrophic earthquake in Haiti; then a massive British Petroleum oil spill dominated the news for much of the spring and summer. Domestically the U.S. economy continued in its slump, with high unemployment.

In numismatics, rarities and $100,000-plus coins were not as active in 2010 as in preceding years, although there were exceptions. In January one of five known examples of the 1913 Liberty Head nickel sold at auction for $3,737,500. Throughout the year several individual coins sold for $1 million or more. Meanwhile, popular collector coins and paper money continued to enjoy solid footing in the marketplace. The Mint introduced its new program of National Park quarters, and companion five-ounce America the Beautiful silver bullion coins (see page 121).

The silver market was active, with per-ounce prices ranging from $15 to more than $30. In late summer the price hit $20 and climbed steadily. Silver averaged for the year more than $5 per ounce higher than 2009. Gold rose as well, more than $200 per ounce, to $1,124.53; and platinum saw a $400 jump to an average of $1,608.98 for the year.

2010 average silver price: $20.19/ounce.

Coin commentary: The 2010 American Silver Eagle was available for purchase later in the year than previous dates. Under a normal production schedule the Mint would have started striking 2010-dated coins in late 2009, for distribution starting in the first week of January 2010. The immense demand for American Silver Eagles in 2009 kept Mint presses running through to the end of December. Production of 2010 bullion strikes was delayed; the coins finally were made available on January 19.

The Mint once again followed a rationing program, as it had in 2009, allocating quantities of the bullion coins to its distributors. For most of the year the Mint also delayed production of collector versions (Proof and Burnished) of the 2010 coins, and the hobby community was uncertain whether any would be forthcoming. These steps were necessary because of the ongoing shortage of silver blanks, and the Mint's congressional mandate to produce sufficient bullion-strike coins to satisfy public demand. Finally, on September 2, the rationing was lifted. (Proofs would in fact be produced in 2010, but the Burnished collector coins would be further postponed until 2011.)

Tens of thousands of professionally graded 2010 bullion strikes have been certified as MS-70.

2010	<MS-65	MS-65	MS-66	MS-67	MS-68	MS-69	MS-70	Total
Certified	5	3	11	38	172	25,019	71,692	96,960
Value					$25	$30	$60	

2010-W, PROOF
Mintage: 860,000

Minted at West Point, with W mintmark

Coin commentary: Production of Proof 2010 American Silver Eagles was far from guaranteed until well into autumn that year. The Mint's situation was similar to that of 2009: a shortage of silver blanks forced all production to be focused on bullion-strike coins. (The legislation that authorized the bullion program mandated that the bullion coins be produced in quantities sufficient to satisfy public demand. When demand was greater than the supply of silver planchets, collector-quality Proofs had to take a back seat to the standard-quality bullion coins.)

Finally, in early October Mint officials were able to announce that 2010 Proofs would indeed be made available for collectors. Order-taking would start on November 19, and coins would begin shipping on December 1.

The issue price was set at $45.95 per coin—a $14 increase over the last available Proof, the 2008-W. Customers were at first limited to 100 coins per household (that limit was later removed), and no maximum mintage was established. Initial demand was high, with the Mint selling more than 700,000 Proofs in two weeks. Ultimately some 860,000 coins were bought by collectors.

No Burnished American Silver Eagles were issued in 2010.

Late in 2010 legislation was passed allowing the Mint to produce collectible (Proof and Burnished) American Silver Eagles even if public demand for the regular bullion coin is not met in a given year.

A large percentage of the 2010-W Proofs that have been professionally certified, graded, and encapsulated are at the PF-70 level.

2010-W	<PF-65	PF-65	PF-66	PF-67	PF-68	PF-69	PF-70	Total
Certified	1	5	3	35	202	21,014	18,401	39,665
Value					$65	$77	$100	

2011, Bullion Strike

Mintage: 39,868,500

Minted at West Point and San Francisco, without mintmark

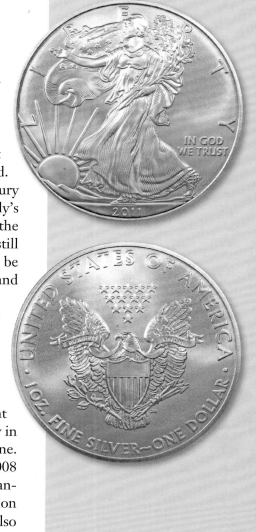

Historical context: Major news stories of 2011 included the death of terrorist Osama bin Laden and unrest and civil war in the Arab world, including the overthrow and killing of Moammar Gadhafi in Libya. In the United States, the continuing economic hard times dominated the news.

The coin market maintained its overall strength of recent years. Most collector items offered for retail sale or put up for bid enjoyed ready demand. A significant numismatic court case reached a milestone in July 2011. A jury decided unanimously in favor of the federal government regarding a family's inheritance of ten super-rare 1933 double eagles. The jury concluded that the coins had been illegally obtained from the U.S. government, and therefore still were government property, and subject to forfeiture. The decision would be affirmed a year later. The decision would later be appealed by the family and the case remains in litigation as of early 2016.

Silver was robust in 2011, with its yearly average bullion value topping $35 per ounce—a 75 percent increase over 2010. Gold was strong, as well, increasing by nearly $450 per ounce, to $1,571.52. Platinum, while not as dramatic, increased by more than $100 per ounce, to a yearly average of $1,721.86.

2011 average silver price: $35.12/ounce.

Coin commentary: Demand for the American Silver Eagle was strong right out of the gate in 2011. Sales of 2011-dated bullion strikes commenced early in January, and more than 6 million of the coins were sold in that month alone. To meet the public demand for the silver coins, which had exploded in 2008 and had been increasing since, the U.S. Mint fired up its presses at the San Francisco Mint to assist West Point with production. It fine-tuned the production processes at the latter facility to boost output. Meanwhile, the Mint was also able to secure additional suppliers for the silver blanks used to make the coins.

In early 2013 the numismatic press reported that fake 2011 American Silver Eagles had come to light in Canada. Paul Gilkes noted that "A counterfeit 2011 American Eagle silver bullion coin recently passed as genuine at a coin shop in Toronto contains no silver, but does contain a trace amount of gold in its composition. . . . It is unknown how many counterfeit 2011 silver American Eagles were passed as genuine and whether fake silver American Eagles bearing other dates are also in the marketplace" (*Coin World*, "Fake American Eagle Silver Coins Surface," February 4, 2013).

The 2011 bullion strikes bear no mintmarks to distinguish which were struck at West Point and which at San Francisco. However, PCGS and NGC differentiate between the two when a San Francisco "monster box" with appropriate markings is submitted for grading.

2011	<MS-65	MS-65	MS-66	MS-67	MS-68	MS-69	MS-70	Total
Certified	6	4	20	100	726	35,191	72,295	108,342
Value, 2011(W)				$25	$30	$90		
Value, 2011(S)				$25	$32	$100		

2011-W, Burnished

Mintage: *309,884 (estimated: figure not audited)*

Minted at West Point, with W mintmark

Coin commentary: In 2011 the Mint issued another Burnished American Silver Eagle—its fourth since 2006—for collectors. (Production of the Burnished collector coins was cancelled in 2009 and 2010 so the Mint could focus all its efforts on the regular bullion strike.) The issue price was established at $60.45 and later lowered to $50.95. The coins have yet to attain a significant premium on the secondary market. In addition to being sold individually, the 2011-W Burnished American Silver Eagle was available as part of the five-coin 25th Anniversary Silver Eagle Set (see page 110).

The Mint announced the coins' release on September 8, 2011. "The United States Mint will offer 2011 American Eagle Silver Uncirculated coins beginning at noon Eastern Time (ET) on September 15, 2011," its press release stated. "The one-ounce .999 silver coin is currently priced at $60.45. As with all products sold by the United States Mint containing precious metals, pricing is subject to change." It then described the coins' production and packaging: "Struck on specially burnished blanks, American Eagle Silver Uncirculated coins feature a finish similar to their bullion counterparts but carry the 'W' mintmark, indicating production at the United States mint at West Point. Each coin is encapsulated in protective plastic and placed in a blue presentation case accompanied by a certificate of authenticity."

PCGS and NGC grade the individually sold coins as well as those they designate as First Strikes and Early Releases, and also those issued in the Anniversary set (identified as such on their slab labels), and First Strikes and Early Releases from the Anniversary set. In order to certify individual coins as coming from the 25th Anniversary Set, the third-party grading firms require the entire set to be submitted in its original, sealed Mint shipping box.

2011-W, Burnished	<MS-65	MS-65	MS-66	MS-67	MS-68	MS-69	MS-70	Total
Certified	0	4	7	46	844	12,738	14,379	28,018
Value					$55	$65	$80	

2011-S, BURNISHED
Mintage: 99,882

Minted at San Francisco, with S mintmark

Coin commentary: The 2011-S Burnished (*Uncirculated*, in Mint terminology) American Silver Eagle was issued as part of the Mint's special five-coin 25th Anniversary Silver Eagle Set. The coin was unique to the set—that is, not available for sale individually. Production was limited to 100,000 sets, which sold out in a matter of hours on October 27, 2011.

For more information on the five-coin set, see page 110.

The 2011-S has been eagerly followed by collectors, and commented upon in the numismatic press. Eric Jordan, writing in *Numismatic News* in August 2012, observed that "Sometimes a mintage listing is worth a thousand words and that is certainly the case with the 2011-S silver dollar" (*Numismatic News*, "Silver Eagle: The Modern Morgan," August 21, 2012). In the third edition of *100 Greatest U.S. Modern Coins*, published in 2014, coauthors Scott Schechter and Jeff Garrett comment on the Mint's reasoning behind this particular American Silver Eagle: "Even with so much enthusiasm about this coin, to many it seemed odd or somewhat arbitrary that a San Francisco–made silver eagle was included in the set at all. Why San Francisco? There are two reasons. First, to Mint personnel, the San Francisco Mint is closely associated with the early history of the silver eagle. In 1986, the first silver eagles were struck there. Proof silver eagles, the only silver eagles sold directly to collectors, were made at San Francisco exclusively from 1986 to 1992. Second, starting again in 2011, San Francisco joined West Point in the production of bullion silver eagles." Describing the 2011-S, Schechter and Garrett write, "Everything else in this set had been seen before, but this coin was truly a first: the first-ever Uncirculated silver eagle with an S mintmark." They sum up the hobby community's excitement at the time of release: "Wow! This was the coin that really got everyone talking." The 2011-S Burnished American Silver Eagle is ranked number 46 among the 100 Greatest U.S. Modern Coins.

2011-S, Burnished	<MS-65	MS-65	MS-66	MS-67	MS-68	MS-69	MS-70	Total
Certified	10	6	4	77	658	15,132	16,927	32,814
Value					$230	$250	$350	

2011-W, PROOF

Mintage: *947,355 (estimated; figure not audited)*

Minted at West Point, with W mintmark

Coin commentary: The 2011-W Proof American Silver Eagle was made available June 30 of that year, with an issue price of $59.95 per coin. (The Mint's price for the coin was increased in September to $68.45 and later decreased to $58.95, to accommodate the changing bullion price of silver.) Collectors bought nearly 370,000 of the Proofs in the first six days of sales, before sales slowed down and leveled off. An established limit of 100 coins per household was lifted after two weeks of sales. No maximum mintage was set.

The 2011-W Proof was available individually and was also packaged in the Mint's 25th Anniversary Silver Eagle Set (see page 110), which accounted for 100,000 of the coins.

PCGS and NGC grade the individually sold coins as well as those they designate as First Strikes and Early Releases, and also those issued in the Anniversary set (identified as such on their slab labels), and First Strikes and Early Releases from the Anniversary set. In order to certify individual coins as coming from the 25th Anniversary Set, the third-party grading firms require the entire set to be submitted in its original, sealed Mint shipping box.

Steve Roach commented on Proof American Silver Eagle values in the September 19, 2011, issue of *Coin World*. "Bullion continues to drive the market, and the U.S. Mint's recent repricing of many of its precious metal coins directly and quickly impacted the secondary market," he wrote. "For Proof American Eagle silver bullion coins, the Mint's price increase from the June 30 issue price of $59.95 to $68.45 on Aug. 29 sent secondary wholesale market prices for 1986 to 2011 Proof American Eagle silver coins soaring from $56 to $66 over just 48 hours" (*Coin World*, "Bullion Keeps Driving Market: Mint Raises Prices on Proof Silver," September 19, 2011).

2011-W, Proof	<PF-65	PF-65	PF-66	PF-67	PF-68	PF-69	PF-70	Total
Certified	3	1	9	86	588	17,471	17,284	35,442
Value					$65	$80	$100	

2011-P, Reverse Proof
Mintage: 100,000

Minted at Philadelphia, with P mintmark

Coin commentary: The 2011-P Proof American Silver Eagle was issued as part of the Mint's special five-coin 25th Anniversary Silver Eagle Set. The coin was unique to the set—not available for sale individually. Production was limited to 100,000 sets, which sold out in a matter of hours on October 27, 2011.

The Reverse Proof has mirrored design elements and frosted fields—rather than frosted elements and a mirror field, as has a normal Proof.

The Mint announced the sale of the special set on October 20, 2011. "The United States Mint is pleased to announce the opening of sales for the limited-edition American Eagle 25th Anniversary Silver Coin Set at noon Eastern Time on October 27, 2011," it stated in a press release. "Orders will be limited to five (5) sets per household for the first week of sales. At the end of this period, the United States Mint will re-evaluate this limit and extend, adjust, or remove it. The current price is $299.95 per set, but as with all products containing precious metals, it is subject to change."

Commenting on the sales trend of collectible coins like the 2011-P Reverse Proof American Silver Eagle, market observer Eric Jordan wrote, "Hotly anticipated coins have a sales curve much like movie tickets. Each succeeding week's sales are about half that of the previous week and between 60 and 75 percent of an unlimited annual sales run will show up in the first four weeks" (*Numismatic News*, "Silver Eagle: The Modern Morgan," August 21, 2012). The 2014 third edition of *100 Greatest U.S. Modern Coins* (Schechter/Garrett) describes the enthusiasm within the hobby community: "Collectors could not resist the allure of the coins that were unique to this set, including the Reverse Proof. With only 100,000 minted, the 2011-P Reverse Proof is by far the scarcest of all Reverse Proof silver eagles yet issued and is among the most highly sought-after of all recent U.S. Mint releases." These factors have ranked the 2011-P Reverse Proof as number 19 among the 100 Greatest U.S. Modern Coins.

For more information on the set, see page 110.

2011-P, Reverse Proof	<PF-65	PF-65	PF-66	PF-67	PF-68	PF-69	PF-70	Total
Certified	0	0	5	21	420	8,880	18,321	27,647
Value					$220	$250	$400	

2011 25TH ANNIVERSARY SILVER COIN SET

Mintage: 99,882

Minted at West Point, Philadelphia, and San Francisco

Set commentary: In August 2011 the U.S. Mint announced an upcoming commemorative set of five American Silver Eagles that would mark the 25th anniversary of the start of the nation's bullion program. The production limit of 100,000 sets—and the fact that the set would contain two coins not available elsewhere—piqued collector interest. Sales started on October 27 . . . and ended on October 27. The 25th Anniversary Silver Eagle Set sold out in less than five hours of frantic, eager buying.

Each coin in the set has a different finish and/or mintmark:

2011, bullion strike, regular finish, no mintmark. The 100,000 bullion strikes packaged in the 25th Anniversary Set were all made at the San Francisco Mint, although they bear no mintmark. Bullion-strike coins of 2011 (minted at both West Point and San Francisco, without mintmarks) were also available individually and in bulk.

2011-W, Burnished. This West Point–minted coin (in what the Mint calls Uncirculated finish) was also available for individual purchase from the Mint.

2011-W, Proof. The standard mirror-field Proof (with frosted design elements) could also be purchased individually from the Mint.

2011-S, Burnished. This coin was unique to the 25th Anniversary Set (not offered for sale individually). So far it is the only Burnished American Silver Eagle not struck at West Point. It bears the mintmark of its source, the San Francisco Mint.

2011-P, Reverse Proof. This coin was unique to the 25th Anniversary Set—not available for individual purchase. Struck at the Philadelphia Mint, it bears that facility's P mintmark. The Reverse Proof features mirrored design elements (e.g., the striding figure of Miss Liberty) and frosted fields—the reverse of the traditional Proof format.

The Mint limited purchasers to five sets per household, and the issue price was $299.95 per set. Sales began at 12:00 noon Eastern Time on October 27, and the Mint's phone lines and Web site were flooded with orders, with most customers ordering the maximum of five sets. In a matter of weeks the sets were selling on the secondary market for double their issue price. Values have risen since then.

In order to certify the individual coins as coming from the 25th Anniversary Set, PCGS and NGC require the entire set to be submitted in its original, sealed Mint shipping box. See the individual coins' listings for certified populations.

2011 Set	
Value	$680

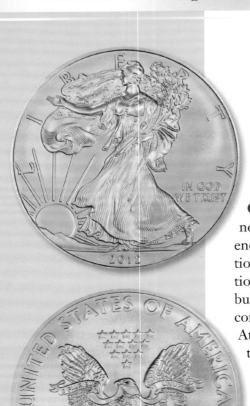

2012, BULLION STRIKE

Mintage: *33,742,500 (estimated; figure not audited)*

Minted at West Point and San Francisco, without mintmark

Historical context: In the first half of 2012, silver was down $3.50 per ounce compared to its average bullion price in 2011. Gold was up about $100 (to $1,660) and platinum was down $150 (at $1,572).

2012 average silver price: $31.15/ounce.

Coin commentary: In a January 2012 article in *Coin World*, Paul Gilkes noted that the year's new American Silver Eagle was among the factors encouraging attendance at the annual Florida United Numismatists convention in Orlando. "An active buying public, strong coin and paper money auction sessions and the first public appearance of 2012 American Eagle silver bullion coins for sale helped bolster the 2012 Florida United Numismatists convention Jan. 4 to 8 in Orlando," wrote Gilkes (*Coin World*, "About 11,000 Attend 2012 FUN Convention," January 30, 2012). "The newest products of the U.S. Mint made a late arrival at the convention but still sold briskly. Shortly after 4 p.m. Jan. 7, two carts—each loaded with 20,000 2012 American Eagle 1-ounce silver bullion coins—were wheeled to SilverTowne's booth on the bourse floor. The Winchester, Ind., numismatic firm was the only company to receive the silver American Eagles at the show. The silver bullion coins, all struck at the West Point Mint, were contained in 80 plastic-strapped, 500-coin boxes. Each box contained 25 nylon-plastic tubes with 20 coins in each tube. . . . Although SilverTowne offered some of the 40,000 coins received as singles directly to customers, most were acquired by customers in multiple rolls and boxes. Abel said it took the firm less than two hours from the time of receiving the coins Jan. 7 to sell all 40,000 coins. The coins were from among 3,197,000 that the U.S. Mint's authorized purchasers placed orders for on Jan. 3 for distribution to secondary market dealers and the public, and were made available for pick up by the authorized purchasers Jan. 6."

American Silver Eagle bullion sales were down in the first half of 2012 benchmarked against 2011. *Coin World* reported that cumulative sales of 14,409,000 coins from January through May of 2012 were 23.7 percent lower than the same five-month period in 2011 (18,901,000 coins). (*Coin World*, "American Eagle Bullion Sales Rise During May: Mint Sales Show Increase After Declining in April," Paul Gilkes, June 18, 2012.)

As was the case in 2011, the bullion strikes of 2012 bear no mintmarks to distinguish which were struck at West Point and which at San Francisco. PCGS and NGC differentiate between the two when a "monster box" with appropriate mint markings is submitted for grading.

2012	<MS-65	MS-65	MS-66	MS-67	MS-68	MS-69	MS-70	Total
Certified	1	9	14	28	91	27,156	55,063	82,362
Value, 2012(W)					$25	$30	$80	
Value, 2012(S)					$25	$32	$90	

2012-W, Proof

Mintage: *877,731 (estimated; figure not audited)*

Minted at West Point, with W mintmark

Coin commentary: The U.S. Mint's original issue price for the 2012-W Proof American Silver Eagle was $59.95, with no maximum mintage established. In an April 9, 2012, *Coin World* article, Paul Gilkes noted, "The U.S. Mint has set a price of $59.95 for the Proof 2012-W American Eagle silver dollar for the coin's initial offering at noon Eastern Daylight Time April 12. The price was posted in the *Federal Register* on March 15. Pricing for the Proof silver American Eagle is subject to change weekly depending on the spot price of silver according to the London PM fix."

The original issue price of $59.95 was later lowered to $54.95 as an adjustment to prevailing silver prices.

Coin World editor Steve Roach commented on the price adjustment in an August 2012 article. "The Mint's recent price decrease for Proof 2012-W American Eagle silver coins—dropping $5, to $54.95—took pressure off of the existing stock of 1986 to 2010 issues and wholesale prices for nearly all Proof issues also dropped by $5," he observed. "The Mint can raise or lower the price of its bullion products to adjust for the price of gold and silver. Perhaps collectors will take advantage of the recent price drop and purchase additional examples to nudge sales for the 'normal' Proof 2012-W issues well past the 500,000 mark?" (*Coin World*, "Proof American Eagle Coins: 2012 Anniversary Sets Still Hot," August 20, 2012)

A Mint press release described the 2012-W Proof: "The obverse (heads side) design of the 2012 American Eagle Silver Proof Coin features Adolph A. Weinman's full-length figure of Lady Liberty in full stride, with her right hand extended and branches of laurel and oak in her left. The reverse (tails side) design, by former United States Mint Chief Engraver John Mercanti, features a heraldic eagle with shield, an olive branch in the right talon and arrows in the left. The American Eagle Silver Proof coin contains .999 silver. The one-ounce coin is struck on specially burnished blanks and carries the 'W' mintmark, indicating its production at the United States mint at West Point. Each coin is sealed in protective plastic and mounted in a satin-lined presentation case. A certificate of authenticity is included."

In November 2012 the Mint announced a new product: the eight-coin 2012 Limited Edition Silver Proof Set, which would include a 2012-W Proof American Silver Eagle. Mintage was limited to 50,000 sets (the original limit of two per household was lifted December 18, 2012), with a release date of November 27 and an issue price of $149.95. At the time of set's release the 2012-W Proof American Silver Eagle was listed as sold out on the Mint's Web site. The new Proof set gave collectors another chance to purchase the coin.

2012-W, Proof	<PF-65	PF-65	PF-66	PF-67	PF-68	PF-69	PF-70	Total
Certified	1	1	7	20	105	7,370	6,740	14,244
Value					$65	$80	$100	

2012 Limited Edition Silver Proof Set	Value
	$250

2012-S, PROOF

Mintage: *281,792 (estimated; figure not audited)*

Minted at San Francisco, with S mintmark

Coin commentary: The Proof 2012-S American Silver Eagle was at first made available by the Mint only in its two-coin 2012 San Francisco Proof Set. On July 19, 2012, the Mint announced that the 2012-S Proof would be available in another set, as well. The coin would be packaged in a "Making American History Coin and Currency Set" along with a $5 Federal Reserve note. The set was promoted as a commemorative of the 150th anniversary of the Bureau of Engraving and Printing and the 220th anniversary of the U.S. Mint.

The numismatic press kept the hobby community apprised on the changing situation. "Surprisingly," wrote *Coin World* editor Steve Roach in a late-August 2012 market analysis, "the U.S. Mint's recent announcement that it would be producing more Proof 2012-S American Eagle silver coins has not taken the pressure off of the 2012-S San Francisco Two-Coin Anniversary set."

The Mint released a statement on July 25, 2012. "The United States Mint is proud to bring to market this year two specially designed sets—the 2012 American Eagle San Francisco Two-Coin Silver Proof Set and the Making American History Coin and Currency Set. The 2012 American Eagle San Francisco Two-Coin Silver Proof Set contains an American Silver Eagle Proof coin and an American Eagle Reverse Proof coin, both with the 'S' mintmark. We provided our customers a four-week window to order the set and indicated that we would mint to the demands that our customers expressed during that period. Sales totals reached more than 251,000 sets. . . . Actual product development for the [Making American History set] was under way prior to the American Eagle San Francisco Two-Coin Silver Proof Set on May 2. The United States Mint, in developing these products, was responding to customers who have indicated an attraction to products produced in San Francisco and having the 'S' mintmark. In retrospect, it may have been appropriate to announce our intentions to produce the coin and currency set earlier in the year or perhaps simultaneously with the two-coin set."

2012-S, Proof	<PF-65	PF-65	PF-66	PF-67	PF-68	PF-69	PF-70	Total
Certified	1	3	6	23	207	11,031	5,868	17,139
Value					$60	$75	$110	

2012-S, REVERSE PROOF
Mintage: 224,935
Minted at San Francisco, with S mintmark

Coin commentary: The Reverse Proof 2012-S American Silver Eagle was made available by the Mint only in its two-coin 2012 San Francisco Proof Set.

The hobby community eagerly followed news of the release of 2012 American Silver Eagles. At first collectors assumed the 2012-S Proof and Reverse Proof coins would both be issued only in the year's special two-coin San Francisco set. When the U.S. Mint announced that a second 2012 set would also include the 2012-S Proof, some collectors complained. "The good news," noted one front-page article, "is there are no plans to sell more 2012-S Reverse Proof silver American Eagle coins" (*Numismatic News*, "More 2012-S Proof Eagles," August 14, 2012).

The Mint's intentions for the 2012-S Reverse Proof were affirmed in a statement released on July 25, 2012: "The 2012 American Eagle Silver Reverse Proof coin will only be offered in the 2012 American Eagle San Francisco Two-Coin Silver Proof Set."

To avoid the disappointment felt by many collectors who weren't able to order the 2011 25th Anniversary set before its lightning-fast sellout, the Mint organized a new ordering process for the 2012 San Francisco set. Sale of the set started at noon on June 7, 2012, and was scheduled to last until 5:00 p.m. July 5. No household order limit was set. The Mint posted sales figures daily on its Web site, to keep collectors and investors informed. "A final and unexpected announcement came on December 6, 2012, that buoyed the spirits of those who had purchased the two-coin Proof set," Scott Schechter and Jeff Garrett write in *100 Greatest U.S. Modern Coins*, third edition. "After the processing of returns and order cancellations, net orders slid back to 224,998, pushing the rarity of this coin ahead of the 2006 Reverse Proof." The 2012-S Reverse Proof is ranked number 87 among the 100 Greatest U.S. Modern Coins.

2012-S, Reverse Proof	<PF-65	PF-65	PF-66	PF-67	PF-68	PF-69	PF-70	Total
Certified	1	2	2	11	168	12,366	5,866	18,416
Value					$100	$130	$200	

2012-W, BURNISHED

Mintage: 226,120

Minted at West Point, with W mintmark

Coin commentary: The U.S. Mint began selling the 2012-W Burnished (called *Uncirculated* by the Mint) American Silver Eagle on August 2, 2012. The issue price was $45.95, with the Mint noting that, "as with all products sold by the Mint containing precious metals, pricing is subject to change." The coins were struck on specially prepared blanks, giving them a finish similar to their bullion counterparts, but distinguished by a W mintmark. The Burnished coins are sold in a blue presentation case accompanied by a certificate of authenticity.

2012-W, Burnished	<MS-65	MS-65	MS-66	MS-67	MS-68	MS-69	MS-70	Total
Certified	0	0	1	1	42	5,132	4,799	9,975
Value					$70	$75	$125	

2012 American Eagle San Francisco Two-Coin Silver Proof Set
Mintage: 224,998
Minted at San Francisco, with S mintmarks

Set commentary: In 2012 the U.S. Mint announced that it would offer a special two-coin set of American Silver Eagles, available for sale for four weeks, from June 7 to July 5. No cap was set on the mintage, with production instead being limited to the quantity ordered within that four-week window. The number of sets that each household could order was likewise not capped. The issue price was established at $149.95.

Each of the two coins in the set has a different finish. Struck at the San Francisco Mint, they bear that facility's S mintmark. Neither was available for individual purchase, although the 2012-S Proof was later made available in another special set (discussed on the following page).

> *2012-S, Proof.* This coin features the standard mirror-field Proof format, with frosted design elements. It was available in the 2012 San Francisco American Eagle Two-Coin Silver Proof Set, and (later) in the 2012 Making American History Coin and Currency Set.

> *2012-S, Reverse Proof.* The Reverse Proof features mirrored design elements (e.g., the striding figure of Miss Liberty) and frosted fields—the reverse of the traditional Proof format. This coin was available only in the 2012 San Francisco American Eagle Two-Coin Silver Proof Set.

"The 2012 American Eagle San Francisco Two-Coin Silver Proof Set is an exquisite collection that captures the essence and beauty of these cherished coins," the Mint said in its promotional literature. "This set—one American Eagle Silver Proof Coin and one American Eagle Silver Reverse Proof Coin minted at the United States Mint at San Francisco—is a testament to the fine, exacting craftsmanship that has been a United States Mint hallmark since 1792."

The Mint updated its Web site with daily sales numbers throughout the four-week ordering period. This allowed collectors and investors to watch the market and gauge when—and how many sets—they purchased. The first day tallied an impressive 85,000 sets sold. Sales dropped off dramatically after that, as collectors waited and watched, but then they spiked again as the July 5 deadline neared. At the end of sales the Mint announced that 251,302 sets had been ordered. That number was adjusted in December, after returns were processed and order cancellations were counted. The final net number of 2012 San Francisco American Eagle Two-Coin Silver Proof Sets sold was 224,998. This made the 2012-S Reverse Proof rarer than the 2006-P Reverse Proof (with its mintage of 248,875 coins), although not as rare as the 2011-P (at 100,000 coins).

2012 American Eagle San Francisco Two-Coin Silver Proof Set	Value
	$200

2012 MAKING AMERICAN HISTORY COIN AND CURRENCY SET

Mintage: 56,857

Minted at San Francisco, with S mintmark

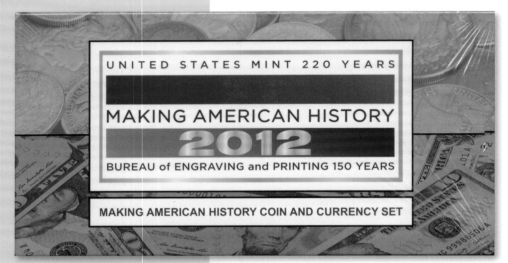

Set commentary: This special set was announced by the U.S. Mint on July 26, 2012—several weeks after the July 5 sales deadline for the 2012 American Eagle San Francisco Two-Coin Silver Proof Set.

The 2012 Making American History Coin and Currency Set went on sale at noon Eastern Time, August 7. It was a joint production of the Mint and the Bureau of Engraving and Printing, marking their 220th and 150th anniversaries, respectively.

The set consists of a 2012-S Proof American Silver Eagle and a Series 2009 $5 Federal Reserve Note with the seal of the Federal Reserve Bank of San Francisco. The serial number of each note starts with the numbers 150. The set debuted at the American Numismatic Association's annual summer convention, called the World's Fair of Money, in Philadelphia. The issue price was $72.95 per set, with no per-household ordering limits. Initial production was 50,000 sets and maximum production was capped at 100,000 sets.

Describing the 2012-S Proof coin, the Mint's promotional literature noted that "This 2012 American Eagle Silver Proof Coin not only honors the artistry and design of our Nation's coins, but also honors the heritage of coin production at the United States Mint at San Francisco." It went on to describe the commemorative banknote: "The Series 2009 $5 note commemorates the Bureau of Engraving and Printing's 150 years of service with a serial number beginning with '150' and bears the signature of Treasurer of the United States Rosie Rios and the San Francisco Federal Reserve Bank designation." And furthermore: "This Making American History Coin and Currency Set commemorates the history and achievements of these institutions and reflects the hard work of thousands of Americans in manufacturing our coins and currency. The beauty and quality of their craftsmanship showcase America's cutting-edge design and manufacturing processes. United States coins and currency exhibit the strength, security, confidence and excellence that are the hallmarks of our Nation."

2012 Making American History Coin and Currency Set	Value
	$80

2013, Bullion Strike

Mintage: 42,675,000

Minted at San Francisco and West Point, without mintmark

Historical context: Silver started strong in 2013 with a January average of $31.11 per ounce. It would fall gradually for the first half of the year before a particularly volatile July when it ranged from $19.10 to $26.40 per ounce. It would end the year relatively stable, hovering around $20 per ounce.

The American economy continued the slow upswing and recovery that had marked 2012. Household debt was down, and corporate profits were up. Home prices nationwide had stopped falling and started to rise, although many families were still recovering from the market's precipitous drop of earlier years. Many banks, wary of repeating the mistakes that led to the Great Recession, remained cautious in lending money. Private-sector employment had been improving since 2010, and this trend continued, while nationwide the *public* sector (from the local up to the federal level) continued its cost-cutting layoffs and budget reductions. Many corporations continued to sit on cash reserves, reluctant to make large investments while future tax and budget policies were uncertain, although increased spending in corporate infrastructure such as information technology implied an anticipation of future growth.

2013 average silver price (first quarter): $23.79/ounce.

Coin commentary: In mid-January 2013 the U.S. Mint informed its authorized purchasers that it had temporarily sold out of 2013 American Silver Eagle bullion coins. "As a result," the Mint announced, "sales are suspended until we can build up an inventory of these coins. Sales will resume on or about the week of January 28, 2013, via the allocation process." Some 6,700,000 ounces of the bullion coins had been sold between January 7, when they first went on sale, and January 15. Business resumed later in the month, and January eventually saw sales of 7,498,000 coins—the single-month record for the series. First-quarter sales continued in that vein, with February (3,368,500 coins) and March (3,356,500 coins) both entering the top-20 tier for monthly sales. Sales for the quarter (14,223,000 coins) beat the previous record (first-quarter 2011) by 1,794,000 coins.

The strong sales seen in the first quarter of 2013 would continue throughout the year. Officially on November 12, weekly sales pushed the calendar-year 2013 cumulative total to 40,175,000 coins sold, establishing a record for yearly sales (though the record would be short-lived and would be surpassed in 2014 and, likely, in 2015 as well).

As was the case with 2011 and 2012, the bullion strikes of 2013 bear no mintmarks to indicate which were struck at the San Francisco Mint and which at West Point. PCGS and NGC differentiate between the two when a "monster box" (with appropriate mint markings) of 500 coins is submitted for grading.

2013	<MS-65	MS-65	MS-66	MS-67	MS-68	MS-69	MS-70	Total
Certified	0	1	1	30	104	69,034	97,747	166,917
Value, 2013(W)					$25	$30	$50	
Value, 2013(S)					$25	$30	$50	

2013-W, ENHANCED UNCIRCULATED

Mintage: *281,310 (final mintage not yet audited)*

Minted at West Point, with W mintmark

Coin commentary: "It's not your daddy's U.S. Mint anymore," remarked *Numismatic News* in an April 9, 2013, front-page commentary. The Mint had announced that it would release a new product later in the year: an Uncirculated American Silver Eagle with an "enhanced" finish made possible by new technology. It would debut in a special two-coin set (packaged along with a 2013-W Reverse Proof American Silver Eagle), and would not be sold separately.

The new format features three different and visually distinct finishes on the same coin. A *brilliant mirrored finish* is used on the obverse in the date, the blue-field and red-stripe areas of the U.S. flag, the lines on Miss Liberty's dress, and the mountains in the background; and on the reverse in the devices held by the eagle (the arrows and branch, the banner, and parts of the shield). A *light frosted finish* is used on the fields of both the obverse and the reverse. A *heavy frosted finish* is used, both obverse and reverse, on the other portions of design elements and on the legends.

The enhanced Uncirculated coins are made from planchets specially burnished by stainless-steel shot, water, and soap. The planchets are fed into the coining press by hand. Each planchet is struck three times using specially prepared dies; the dies are auto-polished with a horsehair brush (to achieve the brilliant finish) and then have their heavy and light frosting applied by laser. The dies are coated (through physical vapor deposition) with chrome to increase their life cycle. After striking, the coins are inspected by the press operator before being released for packaging and sale.

Some parts of the process of making these enhanced Uncirculated coins are similar to steps used to produce *Proof* American Silver Eagles. However, there are notable differences, and the Mint does not consider the coins to be Proofs. Mint technician Steve Antonucci (head of digital process and development at the Philadelphia Mint) remarked in an April 3, 2013, media conference that the automated horsehair polishing of the dies imparts a finish less brilliant than does Proof polishing. Also, the planchets are processed differently and for a shorter time than are the polished planchets used to strike Proof American Silver Eagles.

Coin World reported that the 2013 enhanced Uncirculated American Silver Eagles are not the first U.S. Mint products to feature more than one finish. Multiple finishes were used on the Uncirculated 2012-P Hawai'i Volcanoes National Park five-ounce bullion coin, and also on the one-ounce .999 fine silver September 11 medals produced in 2011 and 2012 (*Coin World*, "Mint to Introduce New American Eagle Finish," Paul Gilkes, March 25, 2013).

2013-W, Enhanced Uncirculated	<MS-65	MS-65	MS-66	MS-67	MS-68	MS-69	MS-70	Total
Certified	0	0	3	3	15	7,668	18,758	26,447
Value					$110	$125	$140	

2013-W, PROOF

Mintages: *934,331 (final mintage not yet audited)*

Minted at West Point, with W mintmark

Coin commentary: The U.S. Mint began accepting orders for the 2013 Proof American Silver Eagle at 12 noon Eastern Time on January 24, 2013. The coin was priced at $62.95. "There is no household order limit for this product," the Mint's media release announced. "Customer demand will determine the number of coins minted." Furthermore, "To ensure that all members of the public have fair and equal access to United States Mint products, orders placed prior to the official on-sale date and time January 24, 2013, at noon ET, shall not be deemed accepted by the United States Mint and will not be honored."

As would be expected, in its promotions the Mint publicized the historic and artistic aspects of the coins. "The obverse (heads side) design of the American Eagle Silver Proof Coin features Adolph A. Weinman's full-length figure of Liberty in full stride, enveloped in folds of the flag, with her right hand extended and branches of laurel and oak in her left. The reverse (tails side) design features former United States Mint Sculptor-Engraver John Mercanti's heraldic eagle with shield, an olive branch in the right talon and arrows in the left."

The Mint also promoted the exceptional quality of these coins and the attractiveness of their packaging. "The American Eagle Silver Proof Coins are struck using .999 fine silver blanks that are specially treated and cleaned to ensure high-quality strikes. Each coin carries the 'W' mint mark, indicating its production at the United States Mint at West Point. The coins are encapsulated in plastic, mounted in a satin-lined presentation case, and accompanied by a Certificate of Authenticity."

As in recent years, orders were accepted online through the Mint's Web catalog (at www.usmint.gov), by phone, and through teletypewriter ordering for hearing- and speech-impaired customers. A fee of $4.95 was added to all domestic orders for shipping and handling.

The Mint sold 258,860 of the Proof coins in the first five days of ordering. Demand for the bullion strikes and a need for planchets for the bullion strikes led the Mint to declare a sellout of Proof 2013-W American Silver Eagles on November 11, 2013. However, because of an inaccurate sales report, on February 20, 2014, the Mint announced that it would offer almost 4,200 2013-W Proofs in its inventory to approximately 780 buyers (who had had their orders cancelled) on a "first-in, first-served" basis.

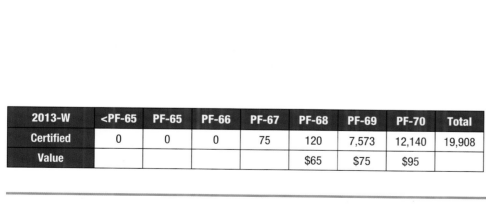

2013-W	<PF-65	PF-65	PF-66	PF-67	PF-68	PF-69	PF-70	Total
Certified	0	0	0	75	120	7,573	12,140	19,908
Value					$65	$75	$95	

2013-W, REVERSE PROOF

Mintage: *235,689 (final mintage not yet audited)*

Minted at West Point, with W mintmark

Coin commentary: The U.S. Mint announced on January 15, 2013, that it would issue a West Point Reverse Proof American Silver Eagle later in the year. The Reverse Proof would be part of "a special two-coin set of American Eagle Silver Coins, both of which will be struck at its facility at West Point, N.Y. The 2013 American Eagle West Point Two-Coin Silver Set (final product name subject to change) will include one American Eagle Silver Reverse Proof Coin and one American Eagle Silver Uncirculated Coin with an 'enhanced' finish. (A 'reverse proof' coin reverses the mirror-like background finish of a traditional proof coin and applies it to the design elements, creating a magnificent contrast.) These two coins will only be available in this special set. The bureau expects to begin accepting orders for the set in the spring. Pricing and other information will be available prior to its release."

As noted in the Mint's announcement, the 2013-W Reverse Proof was not sold separately; it was only available as part of the West Point two-coin set.

To avoid disappointing customers, the Mint had a limited four-week sales window with a sales odometer at its Web site that recorded daily sales. Sales opened at noon Eastern Daylight Time May 9 and ended at 5 p.m. EDT June 6, with the sets offered at $139.95 each. The first sales reported by the Mint on May 10 totaled 138,514 sets. Sales gradually climbed to 182,773 for the May 13 odometer reading; 187,541 for the May 14 count; 191,726 for the May 15 total; and 193,652 for the May 16 total.

Collectors lucky enough to place their orders within the first few hours of release were able to sell their sets at the $180 to $190 level via online auctions on sites such as eBay. At the close of the ordering window, on June 7 the unaudited sales figure for the sets was 281,310. With order cancellations—a result of consumers changing their minds after prices settled down on the secondary market and expired credit cards (since cards aren't charged until the items are ready for shipping)—the final mintage was substantially lower. Later in the year the Mint would lower the unaudited sales number to 235,689.

2013-W, Reverse Proof	<PF-65	PF-65	PF-66	PF-67	PF-68	PF-69	PF-70	Total
Certified	1	0	3	19	173	8,972	17,144	26,312
Value					$90	$110	$130	

2013-W, Burnished

Mintage: *221,981 (final mintage not yet audited)*

Minted at West Point, with W mintmark

Coin commentary: The U.S. Mint initiated sales of the 2013-W Burnished American Silver Eagle on May 28 at an issue price of $48.95 each, with no household ordering limits and the price being subject to change based on bullion markets. Later in the year the price dropped to $43.95 as silver declined in value. Although it sold out individually, the coin was available through early 2014 as part of the 2013 Annual Uncirculated Dollar Coin Set, along with the four 2013 Presidential dollars and the 2013 Native American dollar.

All examples were struck at the West Point Mint on the same blanks that the Mint receives from outside vendors that are also used to strike bullion and Proof examples. What characterizes the Burnished examples from the bullion examples—beyond the W mintmark on the reverse—is that the planchets are specially burnished and they are hand-fed into the coining press. The Mint describes it on its Web site as "a process similar to that used to create the magnificent American Eagle Proof coins," although the Burnished (or *Uncirculated*, in the Mint's wording) examples lack the deep mirrored fields and cameo contrasted devices, having instead a uniform satiny, matte finish.

2013-W, Burnished	<MS-65	MS-65	MS-66	MS-67	MS-68	MS-69	MS-70	Total
Certified	0	1	7	6	52	10,057	24,684	34,807
Value					$65	$75	$90	

2013 AMERICAN EAGLE WEST POINT TWO-COIN SILVER SET

Mintage: *final mintage not yet audited; maximum 50,000*

Minted at West Point, with W mintmark

Set commentary: "Later this year," the Treasury announced in January 2013, "the United States Mint will . . . offer a special two-coin set of American Eagle Silver Coins, both of which will be struck at its facility at West Point, N.Y. The 2013 American Eagle West Point Two-Coin Silver Set (final product name subject to change) will include one American Eagle Silver Reverse Proof Coin and one American Eagle Silver Uncirculated Coin with an 'enhanced' finish. (A 'reverse proof' coin reverses the mirror-like background finish of a traditional proof coin and applies it to the design elements, creating a magnificent contrast.) These two coins will only be available in this special set. The bureau expects to begin accepting orders for the set in the spring. Pricing and other information will be available prior to its release."

The two-coin set honors the 75th anniversary of the 1938 opening of the West Point depository as a federal storage place for silver bullion (similar to Fort Knox for gold). In the early 1970s the U.S. Mint installed equipment at West Point in order to meet increased demand for coinage. The facility produced cents for circulation from 1973 to 1986. No mintmark was used to distinguish these coins from those struck at the Philadelphia Mint (none of which bore a mintmark). In the early 1980s West Point was the producer of the Treasury's half-ounce and one-ounce American Arts Commemorative Series gold-bullion medallions (see *American Gold and Silver,* by Dennis Tucker) and some $20 billion worth of gold was moved into its storage. In 1988 it was elevated to the full status of a branch mint, equivalent to Denver and San Francisco (the latter of which returned from "assay office" status to full mint status at the same time). Today West Point is used to produce some of the U.S. Mint's commemorative coins as well as silver, gold, and platinum bullion pieces. With gold reserves second only to Fort Knox, West Point—unlike other mint facilities—does not offer public tours.

2013 American Eagle West Point Two-Coin Silver Set	Value
	$150

2014, BULLION STRIKE

Mintage: *44,006,000 (final mintage not yet audited)*

Minted at San Francisco and West Point, without mintmark

Historical Context: 2014 was a relatively stable year for silver. Stability combined with affordability led to unprecedented demand for physical silver from investors and collectors alike. As a result, 2014 saw record-setting American Silver Eagle bullion sales of just over 44 million coins.

The Mint was particularly busy producing the National Baseball Hall of Fame clad half dollars, silver dollars, and gold $5 half eagles and a gold Kennedy half dollar. These new coins kept the Mint occupied and no special sets of American Silver Eagles were offered. This gave collectors a break from the proliferation of sets in 2011, 2012, and 2013.

In a March 11, 2014, meeting of the Citizens Coinage Advisory Committee, Chairman Gary Marks announced an initiative to change the American Silver Eagle's reverse design. At an April 8 CCAC meeting 44 possible designs were considered and the CCAC selected no. 41, featuring a side view of an eagle in flight with an olive branch in its talons. U.S. Mint officials informed CCAC members that it would not pursue the recommendation for changing the design. The proposed design would later be used on the 2015 high-relief American Liberty gold bullion coin (see *American Gold and Silver: U.S. Mint Collector and Investor Coins and Medals, Bicentennial to Date*).

2014 average silver price: $19.08/ounce.

Coin Commentary: Although 2014 would end up being a record-setting year, exceeding the 2013 sales total of 42,675,000 coins, the Mint sold just 4,775,000 2014 American Silver Eagle bullion coins in January. This was far from the record established the previous year when the Mint sold 7,498,000 of the 2013-dated bullion coins, setting a monthly sales record that has stood through late 2015. This was because Authorized Purchasers were unable to place orders for the 2014 bullion coins until January 13, 2014.

The late start was a result of the Mint's continued struggle to secure quantities of silver planchets to meet demand. Sales to Authorized Purchasers were suspended on November 5. Sales resumed on November 17.

Authorized Purchasers acquire the coins from the U.S. Mint based on the London PM closing spot price for one troy ounce of pure silver on a given day, plus a premium of $2 per silver coin to cover minting, distribution, and marketing costs. They have a minimum ordering requirement of 25,000 coins for each order placed with the Mint and are responsible for arranging their own pickup and delivery of the bullion coins. The Authorized Purchasers then sell the American Silver Eagles to secondary retailers who in turn sell the coins, described by the Mint as "a convenient and cost-effective way to invest in precious metals," directly to the public.

2014	<MS-65	MS-65	MS-66	MS-67	MS-68	MS-69	MS-70	Total
Certified	0	0	2	2	33	15,042	54,801	69,880
Value					$20	$25	$45	

2014-W, PROOF

Mintage: *940,633 (final mintage not yet audited)*

Minted at West Point, with W mintmark

Coin Commentary: The single-option Proof 2014 American Silver Eagle went on sale January 23 and, as with its bullion counterpart, the Mint saw strong sales in the first weeks of issue. Within the first three months of 2014, total sales of the Proof American Eagle reached 446,373, or more than half of the sales of the 2013 Proof. Through mid-2014 more than 600,000 were sold individually.

The annual Proof American Silver Eagle was also included in a special Congratulations set, first introduced in 2010, as well as the Limited Edition Silver Proof set, which was first introduced as a packaging option in November 2012. The final mintage figure includes the total sales of all Proof American Silver Eagles in all of the product options for the year.

In any given year the U.S. Mint may offer products from previous calendar years for sale, as long as inventory is available. For example, in mid-2014 collectors could purchase 2013 and 2014 Proof American Silver Eagles as part of the Congratulations set, while only the 2014 Proof American Eagle was available individually.

Not all of the 2014 Proofs were offered that year. The Mint offered the eight-coin 2014 United States Mint Limited Edition Silver Proof set—with a 2014 Proof American Silver Eagle—beginning at noon Eastern Time March 17, 2015. That set had a production limit of 50,000 and was priced at $139.95. Mint spokesman Michael White said the 2014 set's release was delayed into 2015 because of packaging issues, and the Mint had made improvements in the packaging based on collectors returning 2013-dated sets.

In a March 6, 2014, blog titled "Mint Stats: Proof silver Eagles move backwards," *Numismatic News* editor Dave Harper observed that sales for the 2014-W Proof American Silver Eagle dropped 9,420 coins to 365,188. He questioned, "Did buyers of that many coins suddenly get cold feet? Without any dramatic swings in the price of bullion, it seems odd. It could be a correction of a previous error in the total. That is one reason why numbers are issued each week." The Mint makes weekly sales figures available on its Web site and through reports that are analyzed by hobby news outlets, and through these collectors and dealers can see the ebbs and flows of the Mint's sales figures.

2014-W, Proof	<PF-65	PF-65	PF-66	PF-67	PF-68	PF-69	PF-70	Total
Certified	0	1	2	19	46	9,612	12,669	22,349
Value					$50	$60	$70	

2014-W, BURNISHED

Mintage: *final mintage not yet audited*

Minted at West Point, with W mintmark

Coin Commentary: Sales for the 2014-W Burnished (called *Uncirculated* by the Mint) American Silver Eagle started on April 10, 2014, at $43.95. It unexpectedly sold out in December, although it remained available in the 2014 Annual Uncirculated Dollar Coin Set that was still available in 2015.

In light of the Citizens Coinage Advisory Committee's recommendation to change the reverse of some or all of the American Silver Eagles, some commentators suggested that the design change be used to revive the Burnished Silver Eagles. In a May 26, 2014, editorial in *Coin World*, editor Steve Roach wrote that although a design change was not needed for the bullion coins ("consistency has given the silver American Eagle a reliable, credible brand worldwide with collectors and investors"), he thought "a new reverse design could be transformative for the Uncirculated American Eagle silver coin," before concluding, "The U.S. Mint has no problem selling the bullion and Proof versions of the silver American Eagle (in fact, it often can't keep up with demand) but a new reverse could make the burnished Uncirculated American Eagle a coin at the forefront of collecting, rather than just another U.S. Mint offering."

2014-W, Burnished	<MS-65	MS-65	MS-66	MS-67	MS-68	MS-69	MS-70	Total
Certified	0	0	0	1	9	1,401	3,697	5,108
Value					$45	$50	$65	

2015, BULLION STRIKE

Mintage: *final mintage not yet audited*

Minted at San Francisco and West Point, without mintmark

Historical Context: In 2015, silver started the year at $15.71 per ounce, jumping to $18.23 in late January. That would represent the high price for silver through October, with the metal dipping as low as $14.27 per ounce in September. Despite the relatively stable price of silver in recent years, due to a surge in global demand for silver bullion coins, the Mint has sought to identify additional suppliers for planchets. Through late 2015 the majority of the Mint's raw-material silver blanks came from two suppliers: Sunshine Minting and Stern Leach.

2015 average silver price: $15.96/ounce (through October 20, 2015)

Coin Commentary: In 2015 bullion strikes were produced at the San Francisco, West Point, and, for the first time, Philadelphia mints. Adam Stump, deputy director for the U.S. Mint's Office of Corporate Communications, said on February 6 that the Philadelphia Mint conducted a "process validation run" of 2015-dated silver American Eagles late in 2014 totaling 70,000 coins. *Coin World*'s Paul Gilkes added, "Collectors, however, will have no way of knowing which 2015 coins were struck at the Philadelphia Mint and which at the West Point Mint, since the Philadelphia Mint strikes produced to date were mixed with West Point Mint output before final shipment to authorized purchasers for market distribution" (*Coin World*, "First at Philadelphia Mint: Facility strikes 2015 American Eagle silver bullion coins," March 9, 2015).

Grading services subsequently confirmed that they would not be encapsulating 2015 American Silver Eagle bullion coins as Philadelphia Mint strikes without concrete evidence that the coins were actually struck there. Since the Philadelphia Mint strikes were shipped to Authorized Purchasers in boxes with West Point Mint strap labels, these Philadelphia strikes are likely to be forever comingled with the West Point examples.

On July 7 the Mint suspended sales of 2015 American Silver Eagle bullion coins to replenish inventory as sales exceeded the Mint's ability to strike coins to meet demand. Sales resumed on July 27, three weeks later. In a September 14 article in *Coin World*, Stump was quoted as stating, "The demand for American Eagle silver bullion coins has continued to increase throughout calendar year 2015 and remains on a record-setting pace," adding, "This demand is a global one and all mints are trying to meet the demand for this precious metal" (*Coin World*, "Silver American Eagles remain on allocation," September 14, 2015).

The monthly sales-figures report that January saw 5,530,000 coins sold. Through mid-October 2015 that number has stood as the highest monthly sales, although July's total of 5,529,000 fell just 1,000 coins short. With a sales figure of 38,759,000 through mid-October 2015, the Mint may beat its yearly American Silver Eagle bullion coins record set in 2014.

2015	<MS-65	MS-65	MS-66	MS-67	MS-68	MS-69	MS-70	Total
Certified	0	0	0	9	35	12,702	26,270	39,016
Value					$20	$25	$45	

2015-W, PROOF

Mintage: *final mintage not yet audited*

Minted at West Point, with W mintmark

Coin Commentary: Sales for the 2015 Proof American Silver Eagle began on January 2 at $48.95 each with no household ordering limits or mintage limits. It was the first coin available in the Mint's 2015 numismatic program, which by the year's end would include more than 130 different products—individual coins, annual sets, special sets, new medals, and the like.

Collectors could buy examples online, or in person at the Philadelphia and Denver mints and the sales center at Mint headquarters in Washington. Examples were also made available for purchase directly from the U.S. Mint at the Florida United Numismatists convention in Orlando, January 8 to 11.

Officials from the Mint worked with several major dealers to make sure that collectors had an opportunity to purchase examples—the only 2015-dated coins then available for purchase—at the FUN show. In a statement released on December 29, 2014, the Mint wrote, "In order to ensure that we have adequate product available for the broadest range of customers possible for the duration of the FUN Show, we reached out to three of our bulk dealers who we know typically attend these events and tend to clear us out of available product stock in short order."

2014-W, Proof	<PF-65	PF-65	PF-66	PF-67	PF-68	PF-69	PF-70	Total
Certified	0	1	3	3	32	2,731	19,775	22,545
Value					$50	$60	$70	

2015-W, Burnished

Mintage: *final mintage not yet audited*

Minted at West Point, with W mintmark

Coin Commentary: The 2015-W Burnished (or *Uncirculated*) American Silver Eagle went on sale March 26 at an initial price of $39.95 with no household or product ordering limits.

In contrast to the distribution of bullion issues, the U.S. Mint sells Proof and "Burnished Uncirculated" coins to the public through its direct-sales channels. While the Mint calls the collectible American Silver Eagles "Uncirculated," collectors most often call them "Burnished Uncirculated"—a descriptive phrase not used by the Mint. However, it serves to distinguish these issues, which look similar to the bullion issues, with the key difference being the W mintmark on the reverse.

Scott Schechter, coauthor of *100 Greatest U.S. Modern Coins*, wrote in his "Making Moderns" column in the March 10, 2014, issue of *Coin World*, wrote that the burnishing process "does not affect the appearance of the coin in any way."

2014-W, Burnished	<MS-65	MS-65	MS-66	MS-67	MS-68	MS-69	MS-70	Total
Certified	0	0	0	0	2	1,405	12,176	13,583
Value					$40	$50	$65	

4

Other U.S. Bullion Coins and Medals

AMERICAN ARTS COMMEMORATIVE SERIES MEDALS (1980–1984)

As described in chapter 1, from 1980 to 1984 the U.S. Mint struck congressionally mandated gold bullion pieces at the West Point bullion depository. These were intended to compete with the South African Krugerrand and the Canadian Maple Leaf. Unlike those coins, the "American Arts Commemorative Series" medals were not legal tender; in fact, they were at first designed specifically not to resemble federal coinage. For the first two years, the medals' edges were not reeded and they bore no marks of fineness or weight. (Half-ounce and one-ounce varieties, in .900 fine gold, were issued each year throughout the series.)

According to the November 1978 legislation that authorized them, the medals (or "medallions," as the Treasury referred to them) were to be "sold to the general public at a competitive price equal to the free market value of the gold contained therein plus the cost of manufacture, including labor, materials, dies, use of machinery, and overhead expenses including marketing costs."

Sales were sluggish at the start. In 1982 the medals were redesigned with coinlike denticles and edge reeding, and near the end of production new marketing efforts were launched. Despite these efforts, sales throughout the series remained lackluster. For an in-depth study of the American Arts gold medallions, see *American Gold and Silver: U.S. Mint Collector and Investor Coins and Medals, Bicentennial to Date* (Tucker).

Examples of the American Arts gold medallions.

1980, Grant Wood. One ounce; designed by Frank Gasparro, with a facing portrait of Iowa artist Grant Wood (1891–1942) and a rendering of his most famous painting—one of the most widely recognized works of 20th-century art, *American Gothic.*

1980, Marian Anderson. One-half ounce; designed by Frank Gasparro, showing contralto singer Marian Anderson (1897–1993) and a pair of hands holding the globe, with the legend UNITY GOD'S WAY, reflecting Anderson's role as a goodwill ambassador of song.

1981, Mark Twain. One ounce; designed by Matthew Peloso, showing a facing portrait of writer and social commentator Mark Twain (1835–1910), and a steamboat on the Mississippi River, reminiscent of his memorable tales set in the American South.

1981, Willa Cather. One-half ounce; designed by Sherl Joseph Winter, picturing author Willa Cather (1873–1947) and a woman working with a field plow, evocative of Cather's native Nebraska prairie, the setting of some of her most memorable works.

1982, Louis Armstrong. One ounce; designed by John Mercanti, featuring jazz musician and singer Louis Armstrong (1901–1971) and a trumpet and musical notes, with the legend AMBASSADOR OF JAZZ.

1982, Frank Lloyd Wright. One-half ounce; designed by Edgar J. Steever, showing architect Frank Lloyd Wright (1867–1959) and architectural masterpiece Fallingwater with a stream in the foreground.

1983, Robert Frost. One ounce; designed by Philip Fowler, with a portrait of poet Robert Frost (1874–1963) and several lines from his famous 1916 poem, "The Road Not Taken."

1983, Alexander Calder. One-half ounce; designed by Michael Iacocca, featuring artist and sculptor Alexander Calder (1898–1976) and one of his famous kinetic sculptures.

1984, Helen Hayes. One ounce; designed by John Mercanti, showing stage, film, and television actress Helen Hayes (1900–1993), with the traditional Greek masks of Drama and Comedy.

1984, John Steinbeck. One-half ounce; designed by John Mercanti and Philip Fowler, with a facing portrait of writer John Steinbeck (1902–1968) and a farm scene hearkening to the rural agricultural settings that characterize some of his most popular works.

Since the United States launched its modern bullion-coin program in 1986, American Silver Eagles have been joined by other silver, gold, and platinum series that give investors convenient vehicles to add physical bullion to their portfolios. Like the Silver Eagles, these coins are also collected by hobbyists, with the Mint offering special finishes and formats for most of the series. Palladium bullion coins and collector coins have been considered for possible future production.

Proofs are created in a specialized minting process: a polished coin blank is manually fed into a press fitted with special dies; the blank is struck multiple times "so the softly frosted yet detailed images seem to float above a mirror-like field" (per Mint literature); a white-gloved inspector scrutinizes the coin; and it is then sealed in a protective plastic capsule and mounted in a satin-lined velvet presentation case (or similar special packaging) along with a certificate of authenticity.

Members of the public can purchase Proof American Silver Eagles directly from the Mint, at fixed prices.

Burnished (called *Uncirculated* by the Mint) coins are also sold directly to the public. These coins are distinguished from regular bullion strikes typically by a W mintmark (for West Point), and by their distinctive finish (the result of burnished coin blanks). Their blanks are individually fed by hand into specially adapted coining presses. After striking, each Burnished specimen is carefully inspected, encapsulated in plastic, and packaged along with a certificate of authenticity.

"Enhanced" Uncirculated American Silver Eagles debuted in 2013. These feature three different finishes on various parts of the coin.

Regular bullion-strike coins are bought in bulk by Mint-authorized purchasers (wholesalers, brokerage companies, precious-metal firms, coin dealers, and participating banks). These authorized purchasers in turn sell them to secondary retailers, who then make them available to the general public. Authorized purchasers are required to meet financial and professional criteria, attested to by an internationally accepted accounting firm. They must be an experienced and established market-maker in bullion coins; provide a liquid two-way market for the coins; be audited annually; have an established and broad retail-customer base for distribution; and have a tangible net worth of $5 million (for silver) or $50 million (for gold and platinum). Authorized purchasers of gold must have sold more than 100,000 ounces of gold bullion coins over any 12-month period since 1990. For gold and platinum, the initial order must be for at least 1,000 ounces, with reorders in increments of 500 ounces. For American Eagles, an authorized purchaser's cost is based on the market value of the bullion, plus a premium to cover minting, distribution, and other overhead expenses. For Silver Eagles, the premium is $1.50 per coin. For gold, the premiums are 3% (for the one-ounce coin), 5% (1/2 ounce), 7% (1/4 ounce), and 9% (1/10 ounce). For platinum: 4% (for the one-ounce coin), 6% (1/2 ounce), 10% (1/4 ounce), and 15% (1/10 ounce).

AMERICA THE BEAUTIFUL SILVER BULLION COINS (2010–2021)

Various designers; weight 155.517 grams; composition .999 silver, .001 copper (net weight 5 ounces pure silver); diameter 76.2 mm; lettered edge; mint: Philadelphia.

History. From 2010 through 2021 the U.S. Mint is issuing a special series of quarter dollars for circulation. Each features a national park, forest, landmark, or other historic site from one of the 50 states, the District of Columbia, or the five U.S. territories.

In conjunction with these National Park quarters, the Mint is issuing large silver-bullion coins based on each of the "America the Beautiful" program's circulation-strike coins. The coinage dies are cut on a CNC milling machine, bypassing a hubbing operation, which results in finer details than seen on the smaller quarter dollars. The bullion coins are made of .999 fine silver, have a diameter of three inches, and weigh a hefty five ounces. Interestingly, they carry the same face value as their pocket-change counterparts: 25 cents. The fineness and weight are incused on each coin's edge. The Mint's German-made Gräbener press strikes 22 coins per minute, with two strikes per coin at 450 to 500 metric tons of pressure.

These coins have all been struck as bullion and also offered in Burnished format.

For an in-depth study of the history, design, production, and distribution of these coins, see *American Gold and Silver: U.S. Mint Collector and Investor Coins and Medals, Bicentennial to Date* (Tucker).

Availability. The National Park silver bullion coins are distributed through commercial channels similar to those for the Mint's American Silver Eagle coins. Burnished coins are sold directly by the Mint to collectors. Production of the 2010 coins was delayed (finally starting September 21 of that year) as the Mint worked out the technical details of striking such a large product. Production and distribution have been smoother since.

AMERICAN GOLD EAGLE BULLION COINS (1986 TO DATE)

Designers Augustus Saint-Gaudens (obverse) and Miley Busiek (reverse); composition .9167 gold, .03 silver, .0533 copper; reeded edge; mints: Philadelphia, West Point.

Weights and diameters: $5 1/10 oz., 3.393 grams, 16.5 mm; $10 1/4 oz., 8.483 grams, 22 mm; $25 1/2 oz., 16.966 grams, 27 mm; $50 1 oz., 33.931 grams, 32.7 mm.

History. American Eagle gold bullion coins are made in four denominations: $5 (1/10 ounce pure gold), $10 (1/4 ounce), $25 (1/2 ounce), and $50 (1 ounce). Each shares the same obverse and reverse designs: a modified rendition of Augustus Saint-Gaudens's famous Liberty (as depicted on the double eagle of 1907 to 1933), and a "family of eagles" motif by sculptor Miley Tucker-Frost (nee Busiek). From 1986 to 1991 the obverse bore a Roman numeral date, similar to the first Saint-Gaudens double eagles of 1907; this was changed to Arabic dating in 1992. The coins are legal tender—with weight, content, and purity guaranteed by the federal government—and are produced from gold mined in the United States. Investors can include them in their individual retirement accounts.

"American Eagles use the durable 22-karat standard established for gold circulating coinage over 350 years ago," notes the U.S. Mint. "They contain their stated amount of pure gold, plus small amounts of alloy. This creates harder coins that resist scratching and marring, which can diminish resale value."

Since the Bullion Coin Program started in 1986, these gold pieces have been struck in Philadelphia and West Point, in various formats similar to those of the American Silver Eagles—regular bullion strikes, Burnished, Proof, and Reverse Proof. Unlike their silver counterparts, none of the American Eagle gold coins have been struck at San Francisco.

In addition to individual coins, American Eagle gold bullion coins have been issued in various sets.

For more information, see *American Gold and Platinum Eagles*, by Edmund Moy, retired director of the U.S. Mint.

Design common to all denominations.

Striking and Sharpness. Striking is generally sharp. The key elements to check on the obverse are Liberty's chest and left knee, and the open fields.

Availability. American Eagles are the most popular gold-coin investment vehicle in the United States. The coins are readily available in the numismatic marketplace as well as from participating banks, investment firms, and other non-numismatic channels. Rarities within the program include a 1999-W $5 coin made from unpolished Proof coinage dies (resulting in a regular bullion-strike coin bearing a W mintmark, usually reserved for Proofs), and a similar error in the $10 (1/4-ounce) series. Among the $25 coins there are several lower-mintage years among the earlier dates. The Burnished coins of various years have smaller mintages than regular issues in all denominations.

Mintmark location.

The Reverse Proof $50 coin of 2006 was issued to mark the 20th anniversary of the Bullion Coinage Program; it has brilliant devices, with frosted background fields (rather than the typical Proof format of frosted devices and mirror-like backgrounds). Fewer than 10,000 were minted, making it a key date in the series.

Design common to all denominations.

AMERICAN BUFFALO .9999 FINE GOLD BULLION COINS (2006 TO DATE)

Designer James Earle Fraser; composition .9999 gold; reeded edge; mint: West Point. Weights and diameters: $5 1/10 oz., 3.393 grams, 16.5 mm; $10 1/4 oz., 8.483 grams, 22 mm; $25 1/2 oz., 16.966 grams, 27 mm; $50 1 oz., 31.108 grams, 32.7 mm.

History. American Buffalo gold bullion coins, authorized by Congress in 2005 and produced since 2006, are the first 24-karat (.9999 fine) gold coins made by the U.S. Mint. They are coined, by mandate, of gold derived from newly mined sources in America. They feature an adaptation of James Earle Fraser's iconic Indian Head / Buffalo design, first used on circulating five-cent pieces of 1913 to 1938.

Only 1-ounce ($50 face value) coins were struck in the American Buffalo program's first two years, 2006 and 2007. In 2008 only, the Mint expanded the coinage to include fractional pieces of 1/2 ounce ($25), 1/4 ounce ($10), and 1/10-ounce ($5), in various finishes, individually and in sets.

The coins are legal tender, with weight, content, and purity guaranteed by the federal government. Investors can include them in some individual retirement accounts. Proofs and Burnished (*Uncirculated*, in the Mint's wording) pieces undergo special production processes, similar to the American Eagle gold-bullion coinage, and can be purchased directly from the Mint. Regular bullion-strike pieces are distributed through a network of authorized distributors. All American Buffalo gold bullion coins (Proof, Burnished, and regular bullion pieces) are struck at the U.S. Mint's West Point facility.

For an in-depth study of the history, design, production, and distribution of these coins, see *American Gold and Silver: U.S. Mint Collector and Investor Coins and Medals, Bicentennial to Date* (Tucker).

Striking and Sharpness. Striking is generally sharp.

Availability. American Buffalo .9999 fine gold bullion coins are a popular way to buy and sell 24-karat gold. The coins are readily available in the numismatic marketplace as well as from participating banks, investment firms, and other non-numismatic channels. Mintages range from less than 10,000 to more than 300,000 pieces, with the Burnished versions being the rarest.

FIRST SPOUSE $10 GOLD BULLION COINS (2007–2016)

Various designers; weight 15.6 grams; composition .9999 gold; diameter 26.5 mm; reeded edge; mint: West Point.

History. The U.S. Mint's First Spouse bullion coins are struck in .9999 fine (24-karat) gold. Each weighs one-half ounce and bears a nominal face value of $10. The coins honor the nation's First Ladies on the same schedule as the Mint's Presidential dollars program, running from 2007 to 2016. Each coin features a portrait on the obverse, and on the reverse a unique design symbolic of the spouse's life and work. In cases where a president held office widowed or unmarried, the coin bears "an obverse image emblematic of Liberty as depicted on a circulating coin of that era and a reverse image emblematic of themes of that president's life." The exception is the coin for the presidency of Chester Alan Arthur, which honors suffragette Alice Paul. The First Spouse gold coins are all available in collectible Burnished and Proof formats, with no bullion strikes as such. All were produced at the West Point Mint.

American Gold and Silver: U.S. Mint Collector and Investor Coins and Medals, Bicentennial to Date (Tucker) gives a detailed study of the nearly 80 different coin designs and formats in this series—their history, motifs, production, distribution, and more.

Striking and Sharpness. Striking is generally sharp.

Availability. These coins are readily available in the numismatic marketplace. They were sold directly to the public by the Mint, rather than being distributed through the Mint's network of Authorized Purchasers. In 2007 the coins' mintages were just under 20,000 each. Those quantities dropped dramatically in subsequent years, with 2008 mintages in the 3,000 to 8,000 range, and several 2009 mintages hovering around 2,000. There was a surge of new interest in the series in 2015 with the release of the popular Jackie Kennedy coin.

The first coin in the First Spouse series.

MMIX Ultra High Relief Gold Coin (2009)

Designer Augustus Saint-Gaudens; weight 31.101 grams; composition .9999 gold (actual gold weight 1 oz.); diameter 27 mm; lettered edge; mint: Philadelphia.

History. In 2009 the U.S. Mint produced a modern collector's version of the first Saint-Gaudens double eagle. When the original debuted in 1907, the Mint had been unable to strike large quantities for circulation—the ultra high relief design was artistic, but difficult to coin. (It was modified later in 1907 to a lower relief suitable for commercial production.) Just over 100 years later, the 2009 version was a showcase coin: a tangible demonstration of the Mint's 21st-century ability to combine artistry and technology to make an outstanding numismatic treasure.

Like its predecessor, the new coin was dated in Roman numerals (with 2009 as MMIX). The Mint digitally mapped Saint-Gaudens's original plasters and used the results in the die-making process. The date was changed, and four additional stars were inserted, to represent the nation's current 50 states. Augustus Saint-Gaudens's striding Liberty occupied the obverse. On the reverse was his flying eagle, with the addition of IN GOD WE TRUST, a motto not used in the original design. The 2009 version was made in a smaller diameter (27 mm instead of 34) and composed of 24-karat (.9999 fine) gold, thus making it easier to strike and stay true to the ultra high relief design.

As with other bullion products of the U.S. Mint, the coins are legal tender and their weight, content, and purity are guaranteed by the federal government. They were packaged in a fancy mahogany box and sold directly to the public, instead of through a network of distributors.

The MMIX Ultra High Relief gold coin was ranked no. 16 among the 100 Greatest U.S. Modern Coins (in the book of the same title). "The coin was

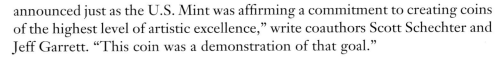

Photographed at an angle to show the edge (lettered E PLURIBUS UNUM), the thickness (4 mm), and the depth of relief.

announced just as the U.S. Mint was affirming a commitment to creating coins of the highest level of artistic excellence," write coauthors Scott Schechter and Jeff Garrett. "This coin was a demonstration of that goal."

For more information about the MMIX Ultra High Relief gold coin, see *American Gold and Silver: U.S. Mint Collector and Investor Coins and Medals, Bicentennial to Date* (Tucker).

Striking and Sharpness. Striking is sharp.

Availability. The coins are available in the numismatic marketplace for a premium above their gold bullion value. Some 115,000 coins were minted.

AMERICAN LIBERTY HIGH RELIEF GOLD COIN (2015)

Designers Justin Kunz (obverse) and Paul C. Balan (reverse); weight 31 grams; composition .9999 gold (actual gold weight 1 oz.); diameter 30.6 mm; reeded edge; mint: West Point.

History. The 2015 American Liberty gold coin, struck in high relief, was intended to continue the era of impressive new bullion coins that started with the MMIX Ultra High Relief. The U.S. Mint described it as "a piece that renders contemporary designs using the latest in modern digital and manufacturing technology." It features the designs of two Artistic Infusion Program artists: Justin Kunz created a modern depiction of Miss Liberty for the obverse, "evoking the ideals of liberty, courage, and hope," and Paul C. Balan designed an American eagle rising in flight, "gripping a branch in its talons as an embodiment of freedom."

In-depth information about this coin is in *American Gold and Silver: U.S. Mint Collector and Investor Coins and Medals, Bicentennial to Date*, by Dennis Tucker.

Striking and Sharpness. These coins are generally sharply struck.

Availability. The American Liberty gold coins were sold directly by the Mint to the public. "Sales opened on July 30, 2015, with mintage capped at 50,000 coins and orders limited to 50 per household," Tucker writes in *American Gold and Silver*. "The issue price of $1,490 (which would fluctuate with the weekly prevailing spot price of gold) was about $400 higher than the coin's melt value in the summer of 2015—and $50 higher than the Mint's pricing for American Buffalo 24-karat gold coins. Still, collectors flocked to the innovative new gold pieces with their unique designs." The coins are available in the numismatic market.

AMERICAN EAGLE PLATINUM BULLION COINS (1997 TO DATE)

Designers John M. Mercanti (obverse), Thomas D. Rogers Sr. (original reverse) and others; composition .9995 platinum; reeded edge; mints: Philadelphia, West Point.

Weights and diameters: $10 1/10 oz., 16.5 mm; $25 1/4 oz., 22 mm; $50 1/2 oz., 27 mm; $100 1 oz., 32.7 mm.

Common obverse and original reverse design.

Common Proof obverse.

History. Platinum American Eagles (face values of $10 to $100) are legal-tender bullion coins with weight, content, and purity guaranteed by the federal government. They were added to the U.S. Mint's program of silver and gold bullion coinage in 1997.

In their debut year, Proofs had the same reverse design as regular bullion strikes. Since then, the regular strikes have continued with the 1997 reverse, while the Proofs have featured new reverse designs each year. From 1998 through 2002, these special Proof designs comprised a "Vistas of Liberty" subset, with eagles flying through various American scenes. Since 2003, they have featured patriotic allegories and symbolism. From 2006 to 2008 the reverse designs honored "The Foundations of Democracy"—the nation's legislative branch (2006), executive branch (2007), and judicial branch (2008). In 2009 the Mint introduced a new six-year program of reverse designs, exploring the core concepts of American democracy as embodied in the preamble to the Constitution. The first design is *To Form a More Perfect Union* (2009), featuring four faces representing the nation's diversity, with the hair and clothing interweaving symbolically. The tiny eagle privy mark is from an original coin punch from the Philadelphia Mint's archives. This design is followed by *To Establish Justice* (2010), *To Insure Domestic Tranquility* (2011), *To Provide for the Common Defence* (2012), *To Promote the General Welfare* (2013), and *To Secure the Blessings of Liberty to Ourselves and our Posterity* (2014). The themes for the reverse designs are inspired by narratives prepared by the chief justice of the United States.

The Philadelphia Mint strikes regular bullion issues, which are sold to the public by a network of Mint-authorized precious-metal firms, coin dealers, banks, and brokerages. The West Point facility strikes Burnished pieces (called *Uncirculated* by the Mint), which are sold directly to collectors. Proofs are also struck at West Point and, like the Burnished coins, are sold by the Mint to the public, without middlemen. Similar to their gold-bullion cousins, the platinum Proofs and Burnished coins bear a W mintmark and are specially packaged in plastic capsules and fancy presentation cases.

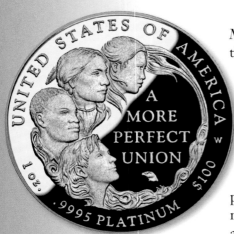

An example of the Proof reverse designs: "To Form a More Perfect Union," 2009, by Susan Gamble.

Regular bullion-strike platinum American Eagles are bought in bulk by Mint-authorized purchasers, who in turn sell them to secondary retailers, who then make them available to the general public. Authorized purchasers are required to meet financial and professional criteria, confirmed by an internationally accepted accounting firm. They must be an experienced and established market-maker in gold/platinum bullion coins; provide a liquid two-way market for the coins; be audited annually; have an established and broad retail-customer base for distribution; and have a tangible net worth of $50 million. Their initial order must be for at least 1,000 ounces of platinum, with reorders in increments of 500. The Mint charges its authorized purchasers a premium above the current market price of platinum, to cover minting, distribution, marketing, and other overhead expenses. The premiums are 4% (for the one-ounce coin), 6% (1/2 ounce), 10% (1/4 ounce), and 15% (1/10 ounce).

In addition to the individual coins, platinum American Eagles were issued in the 1997 "Impressions of Liberty" bullion coin set; in 2007 "10th Anniversary" sets; and in annual platinum-coin sets.

For more information, consult *American Gold and Platinum Eagles*, by Edmund Moy.

Striking and Sharpness. Striking is generally sharp.

Availability. The platinum American Eagle is one of the most popular platinum-investment vehicles in the world. The coins are readily available in the numismatic marketplace and through some banks, investment firms, and other non-numismatic channels.

AMERICAN EAGLE PALLADIUM BULLION COINS (PROPOSED)

Designer Adolph A. Weinman; composition .9995 palladium; edge to be determined; mints to be determined (per the authorizing coinage act: any mint but West Point for bullion strikes; West Point for Proofs, if authorized by the secretary of the Treasury).
Weight 1 oz.

History. In December 2010 President Barack Obama signed Public Law No. 111-303 (the "American Eagle Palladium Bullion Coin Act of 2010"), which required an independent third party to conduct and submit a marketing study to Congress and the secretary of the Treasury. Its purpose: to determine the potential market for a U.S. Mint palladium bullion program. If the study showed that enough demand exists for coins to be minted and issued at no net cost to taxpayers, production would begin within one year of its submission.

The Mint released its 142-page "Palladium Market Study" (produced by CPM Group LLC) in August 2012. The report's main conclusions were:

It is unlikely that there will be sufficient demand for a U.S. Mint palladium bullion coin and such a program would most likely not be possible to undertake profitably.

It is unlikely that there will be sufficient demand for a U.S. Mint palladium numismatic (proof or uncirculated) coin, but such a program could be undertaken profitably.

1. Pursuing such a program alone, rather than in conjunction with a bullion program, may not be in line with the U.S. Mint's usual approach to precious metals coin programs.
2. Pursuing a numismatic program without a bullion coin program additionally may not be in the purview of Public Law 111-303, which directs the U.S. Mint to focus on "the production of palladium bullion coins to provide affordable opportunities for investments in precious metals, and for other purposes."

Furthermore, the report summarized: "The main factors supporting these conclusions is that the potential pool of buyers of palladium bullion and numismatic coins is small and there is little interest in the market for palladium in coin form. The one readily available palladium coin market example is with the Canadian Maple Leaf palladium coin. The market currently is overly supplied, with ample supplies of Canadian Maple Leaf palladium coins available for sale in the secondary market by investors, and little buying interest. The Royal Canadian Mint suspended its palladium bullion coin program due to the lack of demand for the product after 2009, has not made any new palladium coins since 2009, and has no current plans to re-launch the program in the future. There is scope for substantial initial interest in a U.S. Mint palladium coin, but this interest, triggered by the newness of the issue, would likely be transient and unsustainable."

If the palladium coinage were approved, the coins would bear a high-relief rendition of the obverse of Adolph A. Weinman's Winged Liberty dime (minted from 1916 to 1945). The reverse would be derived from the 1907 American Institute of Architects medal (also designed by Weinman).

The palladium used in the bullion program must come first (if available) from natural deposits in the United States (including its territories), to be coined within one year after the month in which it was mined.

 A
Check List of
American Silver Eagles

Use this appendix as a check list and record book of your American Silver Eagle collection. A "Quantity" column is included because many collectors purchase multiples of each coin.

Coin	Quantity	Highest Grade	Purchase Price	Notes
1986 † (a)				
1986-S, Proof				
1987 (a)				
1987-S, Proof				
1988 (a)				
1988-S, Proof				
1989 (a)				
1989-S, Proof				
1990 (a)				
1990-S, Proof				
1991 (a)				
1991-S, Proof				
1992 (a)				
1992-S, Proof				
1993 (a)				
1993-P, Proof				
1994 (a)				
1994-P, Proof				
1995 (a)				
1995-P, Proof				
1995-W, Proof †				
1996 † (a)				

† *Ranked in the* 100 Greatest U.S. Modern Coins *(Schechter and Garrett).* **a.** *Minted at Philadelphia, without mintmark.*

1996-P, Proof				
1997 (a)				
1997-P, Proof				
1998 (a)				
1998-P, Proof				
1999 (a)				
1999-P, Proof				
2000 (b)				
2000-P, Proof				
2001 (b)				
2001-W, Proof				
2002 (b)				
2002-W, Proof				
2003 (b)				
2003-W, Proof				
2004 (b)				
2004-W, Proof				
2005 (b)				
2005-W, Proof				
2006 (b)				
2006-W, Burnished (c)				
2006-W, Proof				
2006-P, Reverse Proof				
2007 (b)				
2007-W, Burnished				
2007-W, Proof				
2008 (b)				
2008-W, Burnished				
2008-W, Burnished, Reverse of 2007 † (d)				
2008-W, Proof				
2009 (b)				
2010 (b)				
2010-W, Proof				
2011 (e)				
2011-W, Burnished				
2011-S, Burnished				
2011-W, Proof				
2011-P, Reverse Proof				

† *Ranked in the* 100 Greatest U.S. Modern Coins *(Schechter and Garrett).* ***a.*** *Minted at Philadelphia, without mintmark.* ***b.*** *Minted at West Point, without mintmark.* ***c.*** *In celebration of the 20th anniversary of the Bullion Coinage Program, in 2006 the W mintmark was used on bullion coins produced in sets at West Point.* ***d.*** *Reverse dies of 2007 and earlier have a plain U in UNITED. Modified dies of 2008 and later have a small spur or stem at the bottom right of the U.* ***e.*** *Minted at West Point and San Francisco, without mintmark.*

2012 (e)				
2012-W, Proof				
2012-S, Proof				
2012-S, Reverse Proof				
2012-W, Burnished				
2013 (e)				
2013-W, Enhanced Uncirculated				
2013-W, Burnished				
2013-W, Proof				
2013-W, Reverse Proof				
2014 (e)				
2014-W, Burnished				
2014-W, Proof				
2015 (e)				
2015-W, Burnished				
2015-W, Proof				

e. Minted at West Point and San Francisco, without mintmark.

Set	Quantity	Purchase Price	Notes
1993 Philadelphia Mint Bicentennial			
1997 Impressions of Liberty Set			
2000 United States Millennium Coinage and Currency Set			
2006 American Eagle 20th Anniversary Silver Coin Set			
2006-W American Eagle 20th Anniversary Gold & Silver Coin Set			
2011 American Eagle 25th Anniversary Silver Coin Set			
2012 American Eagle San Francisco Two-Coin Silver Proof Set			
2012 Making American History Coin and Currency Set			
2012 Limited Edition Silver Proof Set			
2013 American Eagle West Point Two-Coin Silver Set			
2014 American Eagle West Point Two-Coin Silver Set			
2015 American Eagle West Point Two-Coin Silver Set			

B

Illustrated Catalog of John Mercanti's Numismatic Work

This catalog illustrates the U.S. coins (and a sampling of the medals) designed and/or sculpted by John Mercanti during his employment as a sculptor-engraver with the U.S. Mint. "We are all classically trained," Mercanti said of the Mint's staff, in an interview in the December 25, 2006, issue of *Fortune* magazine, "and we demand a lot [of ourselves] because the Mint is known for its beautiful coins. . . . The best part of my job is seeing the finished product—holding the coin in my hand. It's satisfying seeing them all over the country."

Mercanti's work has been featured on silver, gold, and platinum bullion coins and medals; circulating coins (State quarters); copper-nickel, silver, gold, and bi-metallic (gold/platinum) commemorative coins; and a variety of national commemorative medals.

**1970s FBI Director J. Edgar
Hoover medal, reverse**

*The shield of the Federal Bureau of
Investigation surmounts the life and death
dates of the late FBI director.*

**1979 U.S. Mint Director Stella
Hackel medal, reverse**

*A charming view of the Mint director's
native Vermont is the central motif
of this commemorative medal.*

**1982 Louis Armstrong American
Arts medal, obverse**

*This relaxed portrait of the "Ambassador
of Jazz" is from the third year of the
American Arts gold medallion program.*

**1982 Louis Armstrong American
Arts medal, reverse**

*Mercanti featured a trumpet—Louis
Armstrong's famous musical
instrument—on the medallion's reverse.*

**1983 Los Angeles Olympiad
silver dollar, reverse**

*Designed by Elizabeth Jones
and engraved by Mercanti, this
motif features the head and upper
body of an American eagle.*

**1983 Secretary of the Treasury
Donald T. Regan medal, reverse**

*Symbols relevant to Regan's life are
arranged underneath the emblem
of the secretary of the Treasury.*

**1984 John Steinbeck American
Arts medal, obverse**

*In American Gold and Silver, Dennis
Tucker describes Mercanti's "finely
sculpted portrait of Steinbeck, nearly
photographic in its execution."*

**1984 Helen Hayes American Arts
medal, obverse**

*Mercanti's portrait of the famous actress
is beautiful and elegant.*

**1984 Helen Hayes American Arts
medal, reverse**

*The reverse design of Hayes's gold
medallion features the classical Greek
theatrical masks of Comedy and Tragedy.*

**1984 Los Angeles XXIII
Olympiad gold $10, obverse**

*Mercanti modeled a scene of two
runners holding aloft the Olympic
torch, from a concept by James Peed.*

**1984 Los Angeles XXIII
Olympiad gold $10, reverse**

*The reverse of the coin is an adaptation of
the Great Seal of the United States.*

**1984 Vice President Hubert
H. Humphrey medal, obverse**

*This commemorative medal
features a profile portrait of the
late senator and vice president.*

**1986 American
Silver Eagle, reverse**

*A bold heraldic eagle holds an
olive branch, symbolizing peaceful
intentions, and arrows, representing
national strength and defense.*

**1986 Statue of Liberty
Centennial silver dollar, obverse**

Liberty Enlightening the World, *more
popularly known as the Statue
of Liberty, rises in the foreground, with
the Ellis Island immigration center—
the "Gateway to America"— behind her.*

**1986 Statue of Liberty
Centennial silver dollar, reverse**

*Liberty's torch, held aloft, sends its
rays outward; surrounding this motif
is an inscription from Emma Lazarus's
famous poem, The New Colossus.*

**1989 President George H.W.
Bush inaugural medal, obverse**

*A profile portrait of the nation's 41st
president is superimposed on a finely
detailed view of the White House.*

**1989 Congress Bicentennial
gold $5, obverse**

*The Annual Report of
the Director of the Mint
described this design: "a spectacular
rendition of the Capitol dome."*

**1989 Congress Bicentennial
gold $5, reverse**

*The coin's reverse shows a
dramatic portrait of the majestic
eagle atop the canopy overlooking
the Old Senate Chamber.*

**1990 Eisenhower Centennial
silver dollar, obverse**

*Dwight D. Eisenhower is shown
in two profile portraits: one as
a five-star general during World
War II, and the other later in life,
as president of the United States.*

**1991 Korean War Memorial
silver dollar, obverse**

*Featured are two F-86 Sabrejet fighters,
a soldier climbing a hill, and five Navy
ships, representing America's action in the
Korean conflict of 1950 to 1953.*

**1991 Mount Rushmore Golden
Anniversary gold $5, obverse**

*An American eagle flies above Mount
Rushmore, carrying sculpting tools representing the labor and talents of artist Gut-
zon Borglum and his staff, who created the
national monument in South Dakota.*

**1991 United Service
Organizations
silver dollar, reverse**

*This design honors the USO, a
private non-profit group that provides
entertainment and other services to
members of the nation's armed forces.*

**1992 Christopher
Columbus Quincentenary
silver dollar, obverse**

*Explorer Christopher Columbus is shown
holding a scrolled map and a flag in
front of a globe, with his ships, the* Nina,
Pinta, *and* Santa Maria, *in the distance.*

**1992, General Norman
Schwarzkopf Congressional
Gold Medal, obverse**

*A facing portrait of the retired
Gulf War commander is flanked
by legends DESERT SHIELD
and DESERT STORM.*

**1994 World Cup Tournament
half dollar, obverse**

*A soccer player runs with a ball at his feet
in this motif designed by Richard T.
LaRoche and modeled by Mercanti.*

**1994 Vietnam Veterans
Memorial silver dollar, obverse**

*A hand reaches out to touch the
Vietnam Veterans Memorial, with
its thousands of names of the war's dead
and missing in action; the Washington
Monument is in the background.*

**1994 U.S. Capitol Bicentennial
silver dollar, reverse**

*The motif of a shield decorated with American
flags and surmounted by an eagle is based on
the central area of a stained-glass window
near the House and Senate grand staircases.*

**1995 Civil War Battlefields
silver dollar, reverse**

*A quotation by Joshua Chamberlain,
a Union hero of the Battle of
Gettysburg, surmounts a landscape
of the war field's consecrated ground.*

**1995 Centennial Olympic
Games Track and Field
silver dollar, obverse**

*Two Olympic athletes
compete in track and field.*

**1995 Centennial Olympic Games
Cycling silver dollar, obverse**

*Three Olympic cyclists
race toward the viewer.*

**1995 Centennial Olympic Games
Eagle gold $5, reverse**

*A standing eagle bears a banner with the
centennial dates of the modern Olympic
Games (1896–1996); designed by Frank
Gasparro and modeled by Mercanti.*

**1996 Centennial Olympic Games
Eagle gold $5,
"Flag Bearer" obverse**

*An athlete carries the U.S. flag, followed
by a cheering crowd; designed by Patricia
L. Verani and modeled by Mercanti.*

**1996 Smithsonian Institution
150th Anniversary
silver dollar, reverse**

*An allegorical goddess sits atop the world
holding a scroll embodying Art, History,
and Science—specialties of America's
national museum, the Smithsonian.*

**1997 to date, American
Platinum Eagle, obverse**

*The Statue of Liberty is featured
in a facial close-up; this design
is used on all denominations in
the platinum bullion program.*

**1998 Little Rock Nine
Congressional Gold
Medal, reverse**

*In a simple design, the nine
students involved in the 1957
civil-rights case are cited by name
for their courage and bravery.*

**1998 American Platinum
Eagle, Proof, reverse**

*"Eagle Over New England" is the first
entry in the platinum bullion program's
Vistas of Liberty series.*

**1998 Black Revolutionary War
Patriots silver dollar, obverse**

*Mercanti's portrait of Crispus Attucks,
the 1770 Boston Massacre's first
victim, is an artistic conception—
no historical images of Attucks exist.*

**1999 Rosa Parks Congressional
Gold Medal, reverse**

*A globe and the scales of justice
symbolize the importance of civil-
rights icon Rosa Parks, along with legends
noting her quiet strength,
pride, dignity, and courage.*

**1999 American Platinum Eagle,
Proof, reverse**

*"Eagle Above Southeastern Wetlands" is
the second entry in the platinum bullion
program's Vistas of Liberty series.*

**1999 Pennsylvania
State quarter, reverse**

*The central elements are the goddess
Commonwealth holding an eagle-
surmounted standard, and a pebbled
bas-relief keystone, symbolizing
Pennsylvania's status as
the "Keystone State."*

**2000 Library of Congress
Bicentennial silver dollar, reverse**

*Featured is the dome of the
main Library of Congress
building in Washington, D.C.*

**2000 Library of Congress bimetallic
(gold/platinum) $10, obverse**

*The Torch of Learning, held by Minerva,
ancient Roman goddess of wisdom, is raised
above the Library of Congress's Thomas
Jefferson Building.*

**2000 Leif Ericson Millennium
silver dollar, obverse**

*The helmeted bust is Mercanti's
conception of Leif Ericson—
no contemporary portraits of
the Viking explorer exist.*

**2000 Bicentennial of the White
House medal, reverse**

*A view of the presidential mansion
is surrounded by laurels and the
bicentennial dates 1800–2000.*

2001 U.S. Capitol Visitor Center silver dollar, obverse

The original U.S. Capitol and the later Capitol building are featured in a motif designed by Marika Somogyi and modeled by Mercanti.

2001 U.S. Capitol Visitor Center silver dollar, reverse

A heraldic eagle is surrounded by rays and a ribbon reading "U.S. Capitol Visitor Center."

2001 North Carolina State quarter, reverse

From a design submitted by Mary Ellen Robinson, Mercanti modeled a view of the Wright Brothers' famous first manned flight, at Kitty Hawk, North Carolina.

2002 Louisiana State quarter, reverse

Louisiana is represented by a brown pelican (the state bird), a textured map of the 1803 Louisiana Purchase territory, and a trumpet symbolic of New Orleans jazz.

**2002 Salt Lake City Olympic
Games silver dollar, obverse**

*The crystal emblem of the 2002 Olympic
Winter Games sits atop the "rhythm of
the land" emblem and Olympic rings.*

**2002 West Point Bicentennial
silver dollar, reverse**

*This design is an adaptation
of the seal of the U.S. Military
Academy at West Point, with an
ancient Greek helmet and a sword.*

**2002 Ronald and Nancy
Reagan Congressional
Gold Medal, obverse**

*The former president and First Lady are
honored with conjoined profile portraits.*

2003 Arkansas State quarter, reverse

*From a design by Ariston Jacks, Mercanti
modeled a collage of Arkansas motifs: a faceted
diamond, stalks of rice, a sylvan river scene,
and a mallard in flight.*

**2003 First Flight Centennial
half dollar, obverse**

*Depicted is the monument at Wright
Brothers National Memorial in
Kill Devil Hills, North Carolina.*

**2003 National Wildlife Refuge System
Centennial medal, Salmon reverse**

*Mercanti's salmon reverse was one of four designs
in this popular U.S. Mint silver medal series—the
first to use laser technology in their production.*

2004 Iowa State quarter, reverse

*Illustrating the theme of "Foundation
in Education," a teacher and children
plant a tree in front of a clapboard
one-room schoolhouse.*

**2004 Thomas Alva Edison
silver dollar, reverse**

*An 1879-style light bulb mounted
on a base is surrounded by arcs of
light, "emblematic of . . . the many
inventions made by Thomas A.
Edison throughout his prolific life."*

**2004 Dr. Dorothy Height
Congressional Gold Medal, reverse**

*Mercanti's design features the National
Council of Negro Women's building in
Washington, D.C., with the U.S. Capitol in
the background and an inspirational quote by
social activist Dorothy Height.*

**2005 Chief Justice John
Marshall silver dollar, obverse**

*Mercanti's portrait of Marshall is adapted
from an 1808 likeness
by French artist Charles Balthazar Julien
Févret de Saint-Mémin.*

**2005 West Virginia
State quarter, reverse**

*West Virginia's New River Gorge Bridge
and its scenic environment
are the focus of this design.*

**2005 Jackie Robinson
Congressional Gold Medal, reverse**

*An inspirational quote from the baseball Hall
of Famer, who broke the sport's racial barrier
in the 1940s and 1950s, graces this design.*

2006 South Dakota
State quarter, reverse

*Mount Rushmore is the central
motif, flanked by stalks of wheat
and surmounted by a flying
ring-necked pheasant.*

2007 Jamestown 400th
Anniversary gold $5, obverse

*Captain John Smith, English
explorer and settler of Jamestown,
Virginia, is shown with Indian chief
Powhatan in the New World.*

OTHER MEDALS

In addition to the sampling of medals illustrated in this appendix, John Mercanti designed and/or engraved these medals while working for the U.S. Mint.

19xx Second U.S. Mint, obverse (unissued)

1982 Queen Beatrix of the Netherlands, reverse

1983 Fred Waring Congressional Gold Medal, obverse

1984 Leo J. Ryan Congressional Gold Medal, reverse

1984 U.S. Mint Set filler token, obverse

1985 President Harry Truman Congressional Gold Medal, reverse

1989 Mary Lasker Congressional Gold Medal, reverse

1992 Persian Gulf Conflict Veterans Medal, reverse

1993 U.S. Mint Director David J. Ryder, reverse

1995 Rabbi Menachem Schneerson Congressional Gold Medal, obverse

1995 U.S. Mint Director Philip Diehl, obverse

1997 Frank Sinatra Congressional Gold Medal, obverse

1998 U.S. Mint Service Award pin, obverse

2000 John Cardinal O'Connor Congressional Gold Medal, obverse

2002 General Henry H. Shelton Congressional Gold Medal, reverse

C

The Phenomenon of Spotting

As noted in the beginning of chapter 3, white spots have been known to sometimes appear on American Silver Eagles.

The December 17, 2012, issue of *Coin World* featured an article describing the Mint's acknowledgement of the "white spots" problem for modern silver coins. In it, Paul Gilkes wrote:

> During her less than 18 months as the U.S. Mint's quality division chief, Stacy Kelley-Scherer has focused her attention on a problem that has plagued the American Silver Eagle silver bullion coin almost since its 1986 inception—spots. So far, a solution that prevents spotting from occurring has eluded Mint officials. . . . Each year of the program, collectors and dealers of the American Eagle silver dollars have reported spots or blotches on the obverse and reverse, on all finishes—bullion, Proof and Uncirculated—and on coins from all Mints. The spotting is random and can appear as a single spot, multiple spots crossing the field and devices, or in large blotches or patches consuming significant portions of a coin's design.

The article illustrated spotted American Silver Eagles that had been graded by Numismatic Guaranty Corporation of America (NGC), but the problem is not limited to NGC or any other grading service. PCGS has reported receiving American Silver Eagles in sealed Mint boxes (500-ounce green "monster boxes") and opening them to find coins that had already spotted. "We have also graded spot-free coins, sent them to customers, and then had them returned to us months later after they had developed spots," PCGS notes. "There seems to be no rhyme or reason as to why some coins spot and some don't. But it is clearly something that is happening at the U.S. Mint."

The problem is not limited to American Silver Eagles or even to coins from the U.S. Mint. "We have seen the same spotting problem on modern U.S. silver commemoratives and modern coins from other mints such as those of Canada, China, and Australia," PCGS observes. "Our feeling is that it has something to do with the .999 silver composition, as the earlier pre-1965 90% silver coins seldom spot. However, it could also have something to do with the way the planchets are prepared or washed. We are not sure of the cause of the spotting, and apparently neither are the mints of the world."

The major third-party grading services have developed policies addressing the issue of spotting in American Silver Eagles.

PCGS MODERN SILVER COIN SPOT POLICY

"When initially grading modern silver issues, PCGS will deduct for spots that are already evident. If coins spot after they are graded by PCGS, they are not covered by the terms of the PCGS grading guarantee. If you would like us to try to remove spots from your coins by 'dipping' them, we may be able to do that. It is our experience that spots on Proof American Silver Eagles can be removed in about 80% of the cases, but spots on Mint State American Silver Eagles will only come off approximately 10% to 25% of the time. We launched a Restoration Service on January 2, 2013, and for a fee (grading fee plus 4% of the value) we will remove spots, unattractive toning, and other imperfections. However, this fee would be excessive for most modern silver issues so as a service to our customers, we will have a spot-removal service for modern silver coins available beginning April 1, 2013. We are only charging a flat fee of $5 for spot removal on modern silver coins. Note that we cannot guarantee whether our spot removal attempt will be successful. If the spots do not come out, we will still reholder your coin in its original grade. It will just be a spotted coin of that grade. We anticipate that a two-tier market (spot-free and spotted) will develop, much as it has in the past 10 years or so in the U.S. generic gold market. For further information about our spot removal service, contact PCGS Customer Service."

NGC STATEMENT ON SPOTTING ON AMERICAN SILVER EAGLES

"As recently as December 2012 (*Coin World*, 12/17/2012), the United States Mint has acknowledged that white spots on silver bullion coins are a problem, but to date the U.S. Mint has been unable to prevent these spots from occurring. Similar spots can be seen on other silver coins struck at mints around the world.

These spots, which are likely the result of the methods used to produce planchets, can develop over time even after the coins have been encapsulated by a third-party grading service. NGC will continue to grade these coins to the same accurate and consistent standards, but cannot be liable for spots that occur after encapsulation. The NGC Guarantee specifically excludes coins 'exhibiting environmental deterioration subsequent to certification.' These issues include but are not limited to spotting, hazing, PVC, and corrosion."

Notes

Preface to the Second Edition

1. Ganz, David L. "Book Review: American Silver Eagles," *The E-Sylum*, Volume 15, Number 46, November 4, 2012.
2. Golino, Louis. "The Coin Analyst: John Mercanti's Silver Eagle Guidebook," *CoinWeek*, December 4, 2012.
3. Morgan, Charles, and Hubert Walker. "John Mercanti Dishes on His Career, America's Silver Bullion Program, and the Digital Age of Coining," *CoinWeek*, November 5, 2012.
4. Homren, Wayne. "Book Review: American Silver Eagles—The Mercanti Perspective," *The E-Sylum*, volume 15, number 46, November 4, 2012, article 8.
5. Wilson, John and Nancy. "Book Review: American Silver Eagles," *The E-Sylum*, volume 15, number 54, December 30, 2012, article 6.
6. Gilkes, Paul. "Mercanti Co-Authors American Eagle Dollar Book," *Coin World*, November 5, 2012.

Chapter 1: The U.S. Bullion Coin Program

1. "Possible Silver Stockpile Sale Seen as Bullish for Market in Long Run," *Wall Street Journal*, September 10, 1976.
2. "James McClure, Powerful Western Senator, Dies at 86," *New York Times*, March 2, 2011.
3. *National Security Silver Disposal Act of 1983*, S. 269, 98th Congress, 1st session, *Congressional Record* 129, part 1:1050.
4. "Sales Start Slowly for the New Silver Eagle Dollars," *Chicago Sun-Times*, December 28, 1986.

Chapter 2: Behind the Scenes at the U.S. Mint

1. Bowers, Q. David. *A Guide Book of Lincoln Cents* (Atlanta, GA, 2008), p. 43.
2. "Frank Gasparro, 92, of Mint; Art Is on 100 Billion Pennies," *New York Times*, October 3, 2001.
3. *United States Statutes at Large: Containing the Laws and Concurrent Resolutions Enacted During the First Session of the Ninety-Ninth Congress of the United States of America, 1985, and Proclamations* (Washington, D.C., U.S. Government Printing Office, 1987), vol. 99, pt. 1.
4. McAdoo, William Gibbs. *Report of the Secretary of the Treasury on the State of the Finances, 1916* (Washington, D.C., U.S. Government Printing Office, 1917), p. 365.
5. Guth, Ron, and Jeff Garrett. *United States Coinage: A Study by Type* (Atlanta, GA, 2005), p. 95.
6. Vermeule, Cornelius. *Numismatic Art in America: Aesthetics of the United States Coinage*, second edition (Atlanta, GA, 2007), pp. 138–139.

Index